BRITAIN'S FI

SERIAL
KILLER

THE TERROR OF THE AXEMAN

BRITAIN'S FORGOTTEN
SERIAL KILLER

THE TERROR OF THE AXEMAN

JOHN LUCAS

PEN & SWORD
TRUE CRIME

364.1523
L 933

First published in Great Britain in 2019 by
PEN AND SWORD TRUE CRIME
an imprint of
Pen & Sword Books Ltd
Yorkshire - Philadelphia

Copyright © John Lucas, 2019

ISBN 978 1 52674 884 3

The right of John Lucas to be identified as Author of this work has
been asserted by him in accordance with the Copyright,
Designs and Patents Act 1988.

A CIP catalogue record for this book is available from the British Library.

All rights reserved. No part of this book may be reproduced or transmitted
in any form or by any means, electronic or mechanical including
photocopying, recording or by any information storage and retrieval
system, without permission from the Publisher in writing.

Typeset in Sabon 12/15 By
Aura Technology and Software Services, India
Printed and bound in England by TJ International Ltd, Padstow, Cornwall.

Pen & Sword Books Ltd incorporates the Imprints of Pen & Sword Books
Archaeology, Atlas, Aviation, Battleground, Discovery, Family History,
History, Maritime, Military, Naval, Politics, Railways, Select, Transport,
True Crime, Fiction, Frontline Books, Leo Cooper, Praetorian Press,
Seaforth Publishing, Wharncliffe and White Owl.

For a complete list of Pen & Sword titles please contact

PEN & SWORD BOOKS LIMITED
47 Church Street, Barnsley, South Yorkshire, S70 2AS, England
E-mail: enquiries@pen-and-sword.co.uk
Website: www.pen-and-sword.co.uk

or

PEN AND SWORD BOOKS
1950 Lawrence Rd, Havertown, PA 19083, USA
E-mail: Uspen-and-sword@casematepublishers.com

Contents

Foreword

For a few days in the winter of 1975 it looked as though police had unmasked a serial killer whose reign of terror was unprecedented in British crime history. Convicted of three killings, suspected of another eight, Patrick David Mackay was dubbed the Monster of Belgravia, the Devil's Disciple and simply The Psychopath — as well as a few other names — amid a torrent of public anger at the way he had repeatedly slipped through the grasp of the criminal justice system. When the authorities added it all up, Mackay had been incarcerated, sectioned or otherwise detained at least nineteen times before he was finally brought to justice for his horrific killing spree.

It was a case that left the nation stunned, both by the pure brutality of Mackay's crimes and his unrepentant evil. Yet the extraordinary story of this 22-year-old Nazi-obsessive, who hacked a priest to death with an axe and killed two elderly women during a remorseless robbery campaign on the upmarket streets of West London, was all but forgotten by Christmas.

It had been expected to run and run. Among the unsolved cases Mackay had apparently confessed to in prison — but later denied under questioning — was the murder of a teenage nanny on a train and the heinous double killing of a widow and her 4-year-old grandson. He was also suspected of murdering a popular café owner from Essex. While police had taken the initial decision not to charge Mackay with those crimes, it seemed to be only a matter of time before more evidence came to light. But the charges never materialized. Perhaps it was because, despite his alleged gloating to fellow prisoners, Patrick Mackay did not really kill all those people. Yet while he languishes in prison to this day — still too dangerous to be released — every one of those crimes remains unsolved.

Mackay faded into obscurity in the minds of the British public, far more than other serial killers of his era. In fact, as this book will reveal, he has been able to change his name and win the right to live in an open prison — the first step on the road to eventual freedom — without a shred of publicity surrounding the decision. Far from being one of Britain's most notorious inmates, he is not even recognized as being the country's longest-serving living prisoner. That title was wrongly held by murderer John Massey before he was released in May 2018, even though he had been jailed seven months after Mackay in May 1976. Most assume the flamboyant and infamous Charlie Bronson now holds the record, but that is not the case. Instead, it is the forgotten serial killer, Patrick Mackay, who has been inside the longest.

It is worth noting that Mackay may have had some influence over his low profile. Unlike other killers such as Dennis Nilsen and Ian Brady, Mackay is not known to have ever replied to a letter sent by 'fans' or 'pen pals' who would inevitably have sold any response to the newspapers. Perhaps it was a calculated move, perhaps it was a result of poor literacy.

The question remains: was Patrick Mackay really one of Britain's most prolific serial killers, as detectives originally suspected? That mystery is what this book sets out to examine.

It's a question I could not have begun to answer without finding out much more about Mackay's victims than scant literature on the case reveals. Wherever the Mackay story has featured — be it in books, magazines or documentaries — the lives of his victims, and the other victims associated with his case, are all too often glossed over. Yet it became apparent that only by examining who they were and what happened to them could any real insight be gained into whether or not Patrick Mackay could have been responsible for their deaths — and whether police could have done more to bring their killer, or killers, to justice.

For ease of reference, the victims can be separated into three groups: the convictions, the charges left on file, and the unsolved cases.

Of the convictions, Mackay's first identified victim was 87-year-old widow Isabella Griffiths, who was strangled and stabbed at her home in Cheyne Walk, Chelsea. Next was Adele Price, 89, strangled at her home in Lowndes Square, Kensington. Finally, Mackay killed Father Anthony Crean in a frenzied attack using his fists, a knife and an axe in the picturesque village of Shorne, Kent, leaving the 63-year-old's mutilated body floating grotesquely in a bath full of bloody water. The date was 21 March 1975. Two days later Mackay was arrested.

Although he was charged with five counts of murder, Mackay's convictions were only for three counts of manslaughter. The other two cases were allowed to lie on file, meaning prosecutors believed they had enough evidence but a trial was felt not to be in the public interest. The first victim in this group was 73-year-old widow Mary Hynes. She was choked and stabbed at her home in Willes Road, Kentish Town. Second was 62-year-old shopkeeper Frank Goodman. He was battered with a piece of metal pipe at his premises in Rock Street, Finsbury Park.

Finally, there were five unsolved murders, which Mackay allegedly confessed to while in jail, later telling police he was not responsible. The victims in those cases were Heidi Mnilk, Stephanie Britton, Christopher Martin, Sarah Rodmell and

Ivy Davies. Mackay also admitted to killing an unidentified homeless man whose body was never found.

While serial killers are often suspected of killing more victims than their convictions suggest, Mackay is a rare case. The number of unsolved murders attributed to him online and in various documentaries far outweighs the number of crimes for which he was convicted. Although this is the case with other notorious murderers — Peter Tobin is a good example — few have had their unproven guilt taken for granted quite as widely and for as long as Patrick Mackay. It is a situation that, on the face of it, seems almost unfair.

If Patrick Mackay really did kill eleven people, it would make him officially Britain's fifth most prolific serial killer, behind Harold Shipman (215), Peter Dinsdale (twenty-six), Dennis Nilsen (fifteen) and Peter Sutcliffe (thirteen). And it would have made him London's most prolific serial killer at the time, because the Muswell Hill-based Nilsen was not convicted until 1983.

I did not have access to the police files for the unsolved murders, so it would be foolish to pretend that this book could prove Mackay's guilt or innocence beyond any reasonable doubt. It would also be quite wrong to attempt it — ultimately that can only be done in a court of law. But I can point out where strong circumstantial evidence lends credibility to the theory that Mackay killed more than three people, and which cases could benefit from re-examination.

This book also has what I hope is a noble central mission: to tell the stories of the victims in as much detail as possible and to recreate their last moments, in the faint hope that by doing so it may still be possible for them to receive justice. There is still a chance, however slim, that someone may read the accounts here and provide detectives with vital information, or better still a confession. Four decades is a long time, but not so long that the killer, or killers, are inevitably already dead, and not so ancient that witnesses can no longer remember what they saw. Detectives, some of them interviewed in this book, abide by the adage that a murder case is never closed. Let us see if that's true.

Bibliographical notes

The majority of the information about the police investigations into Patrick Mackay has been sourced from more than 300 original documents held in the National Archives at Kew, south-west London, as well as police documents held in private hands. They relate mainly to Mackay's family and employment history, criminal record, witness accounts and his interviews under caution about the killings of Isabella Griffiths, Adele Price, Father Anthony Crean and Mary Hynes.

Further documents about the Mary Hynes and Frank Goodman cases are held in the archives, but they will not be released until 1 January 2066. After unsuccessfully applying to have them opened under the Freedom of Information Act, the powers that be evidently reviewed the status of the files I had already seen and decided to reseal them. As a result, this book is certain to be the fullest account of the Mackay case available for the foreseeable future.

Writing this book has heightened my awareness of the valuable service provided by local newspapers, not just for the present population, but also for historians. It is a sad fact that, due to the lamentable decline in the newspaper industry, the researchers of the future will probably not be served as well as I have been. I have also come to appreciate the services provided by local libraries and their archives, as well as the extensive stash of local and national papers kept at the British Library in London. The *Southend Echo*, *Hackney Gazette*, *Islington Gazette*, *London Evening Standard*, and *Barnet Press* were invaluable sources, without which this book would not have been possible. Fleet Street titles, including *The Sun*, *The Times*, *Daily Mirror*, *Daily Mail* and *Daily Express* all covered the Mackay case in depth at the time and reports from those papers have been vital in helping to piece the story together. They have been referenced where appropriate in the text.

The only previous book published about Patrick Mackay was written by journalists Tim Clark and John Penycate, who were working for the BBC's *Panorama* documentary series and the *Daily Mirror*. Their 1976 out-of-print work, *Psychopath: The Case of Patrick Mackay*, drew heavily on Mackay's medical files, which he released to them in a desperate bid to help his paper-thin defence case. Its purpose was to expose the shocking truth about the many failings of the mental health system, which missed repeated opportunities to stop Mackay. The killer himself also contributed passages from a short memoir written while on remand in Brixton Prison, which allowed him to comment not only on his upbringing and dealings with various institutions, but also on the murders themselves and, later, further crimes he was accused of committing. It has been a key source, particularly for chapters two and three, which deal with Mackay's medical and family history. Although the memoir and many of the details of the case entered the public domain through court papers, documentaries, newspapers, magazine articles and television programmes, the authors of the book were responsible for sourcing much of the information initially.

After finally tracking down a copy, I spoke to one of its authors, the distinguished BBC journalist John Penycate, who said:

> 'We got Mackay's consent while he was on remand to look at his medical files and his legal files so in that way we got to view a lot of raw material. We couldn't interview him because he was in jail, but through his lawyer we asked him to write his memoirs and we quoted them. It was only a few pages and it was all very self-serving, I think he had reached a point where he was trying to get off the hook for a lot of his crimes. He was drunk

or drugged a lot of the time. He could easily have killed people or attacked people and then forgot about it. He was a psychopath and the point of our book was he couldn't be treated or put in a secure mental hospital.'

I have tried to avoid footnotes as much as possible and most sources have been referenced in the text, including interviews I have carried out with relatives of the victims and various detectives. At the back of this book is a bibliography containing publications and documentaries that have been particularly helpful.

I have endeavoured to track down the copyright holders for all of the photos used but it has proved impossible, owing to the fact many of them are most probably dead. I would be happy to include a full credit in the event that this book is re-printed.

I would like to thank everyone who spoke to me both on and off the record, invited me into their homes, met me for coffee or otherwise indulged my repeated enquiries, especially Victor Davies and family, Ray Newman, Simon Dinsdale, Dave Bright and Lucy Brown. I would also like to thank Robyn Pierce and Susan Lucas for their encouragement and help with the editing process.

For ease of reference, I have reproduced the list of all Mackay's alleged victims.

Heidi Mnilk, 8 July 1973 – NOT CHARGED
The 18-year-old German nanny was stabbed on a train and her body thrown onto the tracks.

Mary Hynes, found 20 July 1973 – LEFT TO LIE ON FILE
Mary, 73, was battered to death with a piece of wood and a stocking was stuffed into her mouth.

**Stephanie Britton and Christopher Martin, 12 January 1974 –
NOT CHARGED**
Stephanie, 57, and her 4-year-old grandson Christopher
Martin were stabbed to death at home.

Homeless man, January 1974 – NOT CHARGED
Mackay admitted he threw a tramp into the River Thames,
but a victim could not be identified.

Isabella Griffiths, 14 February 1974 – CONVICTED
The 87-year-old was strangled and stabbed at her home in
Kensington, London.

Frank Goodman, 13 June 1974 – LEFT TO LIE ON FILE
The 62-year-old shopkeeper was battered to death in his shop
in Finsbury Park, London.

Sarah Rodmell, 23 December 1974 – NOT CHARGED
Sarah, a 92-year-old spinster, was battered around the head
outside her home in Hackney, London.

Ivy Davies, 4 February 1975 – NOT CHARGED
Café owner Ivy, 48, was battered to death at her home in
Southend, Essex.

Adele Price, 10 March 1975 – CONVICTED
The 89-year-old widow was strangled at home in Lowndes
Square, London.

Father Anthony Crean, 21 March 1975 – CONVICTED
Father Crean, 63, was hacked to death with an axe at his
home near Gravesend, Kent.

Chapter 1

The Gentle Lady of the Orange Tree

It was almost pitch black by the time Ivy Davies locked up her café and prepared to walk the short distance home, but the darkness never bothered her. It was 3 February, 1975, and *Down Down* by the rock band Status Quo had spent several weeks at the top of the charts, leaving the tune stuck in Ivy's head. With her hands stuffed in her apron pockets, she hummed along as she made the short 200-metre walk along the seafront and up the flight of forty-seven steps to her dainty little cottage at 21A Holland Road, nestled behind two other properties towards the bottom of the street. It was the only building in the road of its type; the rest were pre-war terraced houses that rose up on a steep slope away from the seafront. Above the front door was an upside-down brass horseshoe. Placed there optimistically for good luck, it was a symbol Ivy's neighbours would later describe as a bad omen.

On quiet evenings, Ivy could just about hear the waves in the distance, lapping at the shore of the Thames Estuary. During the day, the sound of seagulls squawking in the sky or perched on the rooftops filled the air. Her otherwise peaceful little street in Westcliff, a suburb of Southend-on-Sea, in Essex, was not a bad place to live, she thought. Compared with her numerous other homes over the years, Holland Road held no unpleasant memories.

Ivy's plan for the evening was simple. Once inside her cottage she would lock the door and make her way to the kitchen. After boiling the kettle she would sit down with a well-earned cup of tea and then think about heading out to the bingo. The divorcee might have been a busy working grandmother but she had an active social life with a close circle of friends and had started dating again, although she still preferred to use the title Mrs rather than Miss or the more ambiguous Ms. Ivy might not have been a classical beauty — with her thick-rimmed glasses and stout figure — but what she lacked in physical attractiveness she more than made up for with a bubbly personality that never failed to win admirers.

But within hours Ivy would be dead, sparking a murder hunt the likes of which Southend had never seen.

Southend was, and still is, a typical British seaside town. Old fashioned, perhaps, but that's all part of the charm. Its backbone then, as now, was the plucky entrepreneurial spirit of its independent business people who managed the bed and breakfast guesthouses, souvenir shops and cafés. People don't go to the seaside for big brand names. They visit because they enjoy the friendly atmosphere and the personal touch that only independent traders, free from the corporate shackles, can provide.

Ivy Davies was very much in tune with that spirit and business was good at her Orange Tree café. Although not as lucrative as it could be during the height of the summer season, when tourists and locals flocked to the beach opposite, trade was lively enough that Ivy could afford to finish early if she wanted to, although that rarely happened. If she ever did shut up shop before her customary 6pm, it was usually to head to her part-time job as a cleaner at a local secondary school.

About three years had passed since Ivy bought out the previous owner Ernest Hasler, a good-natured and generous man who she counted as a dear friend. She had worked for Ernest for almost five years before he retired and she decided to snap up the Orange Tree. Now, Ivy Davies was as much a fixture at the café as the bricks and mortar.

The Orange Tree itself was one eatery in a row of ten other cafés set underneath Shorefield Road, which snaked up from the seafront towards the main suburban and shopping areas of Westcliff. The cafés were built into the brick wall-like railway arches and originally served as coach houses for the area's fancy hotels. Despite the hotels fading out of fashion — and largely out of business — Westcliff still attracted thousands of day-trippers each year. They would wander along the seafront after pounding Southend's 'Golden Mile' of arcades and souvenir shops or stroll up the world-famous pier, the longest in the world at 1.3 miles. Some chose to soak up the sun on the beach across the road from the arches, where it was considerably more sedate than the packed main seafront, further east. From there, they would spend the day popping over for teas, coffees and an all-day breakfast or two. Ivy's regular customers — her bread and butter — were a mixed bunch and included local fishermen, tradesmen and pensioners who made a daily pilgrimage to the café for a meal and a friendly chat.

Six months earlier, Southend's local paper, the *Evening Echo*, described the row of seafront cafés as a 'dreamworld a la France – underneath the arches'. They were still relatively new ventures, owned by a motley bunch of entrepreneurs, all hoping to promote the tourist charms of the little seaside town with big ambitions. A beaming Ivy peered out from the pages of the *Echo*, enthusiastic about life and the roaring trade along the esplanade. The report said:

> 'There's a place in the sun where you can dream your dreams away underneath the arches and eat Continental-style. No, it's not a little café in Cannes or some romantic trattoria in Italy. It's down on the seafront at Westcliff, with the day-trippers and the holiday-makers.

'And despite the continental look, there are no snails or frogs' legs here. The food is English. For the people who run them, it's a place of friendship and smiles. There's none of the cut-throat competition that you might expect. The traders chat to each other about prices and take a philosophical view of their businesses. They reckon that if the café owner next door does more trade today, tomorrow will be their turn.

'For Ivy Davies, of Holland Road, Westcliff, life under the arches for the past eight years has been "marvellous". She took out the lease after working five years at the café. She said: "It's a great pleasure here and especially when people say they have enjoyed their meal. I love it down here. It's my home and all I work for."'

The photo of Ivy grinning from ear to ear outside the Orange Tree while clutching a tray of empty glasses would soon become more famous in the town than anyone could have imagined, and for all the wrong reasons. After the Westcliff café 'dreamworld' was shattered by Ivy's murder, the same photo would be used by the *Evening Echo* on hundreds of posters appealing for information to catch the killer. Some detectives, still pondering the case today, wondered whether the article — and Ivy's hint that business was booming — sealed her fate.

The day 3 February 1975 was no different from any other for Ivy. She opened the café shortly after 6am and locked up just before 6pm. The same old faces came in at their regular times and one or two day-trippers popped in for teas. Her walk home took just a few minutes. As far as anyone knew Ivy had no plans to receive visitors. There was nothing to suggest that she was in danger of anything more than having too much to drink if she chose to go out. But somebody came calling.

Ivy's body was discovered by Madeline, a friend of her daughter Pat, and a neighbour, Stella Zammitt, after she failed to open up the Orange Tree the next morning. They found her on the settee, wearing her nightdress, at 10.30am. Ivy had been beaten around the head with a heavy object and the front room was flecked with blood. The attack had been ferocious but there were no signs of a sexual assault. A ligature was found around her neck, but this did not contribute to her death.

Madeline screamed, alerting the entire street to the horror at Ivy's cottage. Stella also let out a high-pitched yelp and came running out of the house shouting 'Oh my God, there's blood everywhere.'

Later Stella would say: 'Mrs Davies was in her nightdress when I saw her body. We both screamed. She had a cut across her forehead. It looked as if it had been inflicted with a knife.' She was wrong, the deep gash was in fact caused by the edge of a steel pry bar, carelessly left at the scene. Stella said she had heard nothing during the night to give her cause for concern, which raised the question, had Ivy known her killer? Or had she been swiftly and silently overpowered by a stranger? Her body was later identified by another daughter, also called Ivy, at Southend Hospital.

News of Ivy's death sent shockwaves through the small seafront business community. A waitress at the Beachcomber café wiped away tears as she told reporters: 'Ivy always had a cheerful "good morning" for everyone. She had a marvellous trade at the café. She was very popular and well-liked by her regulars.'

Betty Campbell, who ran the Pomme D'or café next to the Orange Tree, said she had known Ivy for seven years. 'Her two daughters helped her,' she said. 'They seemed very happy.' And Ernest Hasler, Ivy's one-time boss and friend, seemed to speak for the entire town when he told reporters about Ivy's much-loved character. 'I still can't believe she would have had any enemies,' he said. 'She was a gentle lady who wouldn't hurt a soul. She was a very lonely person and didn't have any real friends except for me and one or two others. I was driving past the café at closing time. She didn't see me though. It is a terrible blow. I can't believe that such a terrible thing could have happened to such a defenceless person.'

Ivy's loyal customers also spoke of their grief. 'It has really shaken us all rigid,' said Beryl Walker, a regular visitor with her husband John. 'She was one of the most generous, warm-hearted and helpful people you could ever meet. I remember particularly what she did for us at Christmas. One of my parents had just died and we were all in a panic not knowing what to do. We went to the café on Boxing Day and although Ivy was only serving tea and coffee she cooked us a meal.'

Bill Gardham, from Wandsworth, had a similar tale. He and his wife visited Southend for a bowls day but the game was rained off. 'We had a pot of tea and then I asked the lady — I didn't know she was Mrs Davies then — what time she closed. She said if it hadn't been for us she would have closed. She invited us home to have tea and sandwiches and said we could stay a while. She was very kind to us.' Mr Gardham later sent Ivy an orange apron as a token of the couple's gratitude. 'I hope they catch the killer,' he said. 'This is a sad affair to happen to a person like her.'

It didn't take long for people to start speculating about motives and likely suspects. Locals believed Ivy must have been killed by someone she knew and hinted at a dark and sexually-liberated private life. Detectives wondered whether her kindness and welcoming nature had been her undoing. From their mobile headquarters in the street outside the murder house, police began sifting through the evidence. They had not yet disclosed the murder weapon, but for some reason, possibly due to an off-the-record briefing, headlines in the local paper read 'Mad Axeman Murder Hunt' and 'Axeman Could Strike Again'. The sense of urgency was palpable.

The investigation was led by Detective Chief Inspector (DCI) Peter Croxford, head of Southend's CID. Croxford was a tough former merchant seaman and RAF pilot who was born in 1922 in the East End of London. He joined the Merchant Navy aged 15 and three years later won a bravery award for shooting down a German aircraft that bombed his ship 300 miles off the coast of Ireland. The ship was laden with more than £4 million worth of explosive cordite and a direct hit would have meant certain death for everyone on board. Despite several of his crewmates being killed and Croxford sustaining painful burns, he took to the anti-aircraft guns, blasting the plane out of the sky. He was awarded the British Empire Medal by King George VI and the Lloyds War Medal for Bravery at Sea, one of only 520 ever issued for exceptional gallantry. He later received a Queen's Commendation for a police incident where he managed to talk a man armed with a shotgun into putting down his weapon. If anyone was going to bring Ivy's killer to justice, it was the no-nonsense Croxford.

His immediate boss was Detective Chief Superintendent (DCSUP) Alf Mitchell, an earthy 43-year-old from nearby Tilbury, who spoke to reporters at the scene. 'I appeal to anyone who knows Mrs Davies and may have seen her before she was found dead this morning to come forward,' he urged. The appeal would spark a huge influx of information. Meanwhile, Home Office pathologist Dr James Cameron was already examining Ivy's fatal injuries.

The following day, Croxford released further details about her murder. The Orange Tree had been locked up at 5.45pm. There was no sign of a break-in or a struggle at Holland Road, which suggested Ivy knew her killer. She may have been wearing a 'greenish-blue' dress when she was last seen in public, but detectives wanted to speak to anyone who knew what Ivy did in her spare time. They knew she was seen occasionally at Southend's Talk of the South nightclub. They confirmed that she was divorced and her ex-husband lived in Wales. The post-mortem revealed Ivy died from multiple head injuries.

That day's paper carried a photo of the café, which had now been padlocked – a striking visual metaphor for Ivy's untimely fate. Police dogs were brought in to search land belonging to the former Coast Hotel, directly behind Ivy's cottage. Uniformed officers conducted a fingertip search of the area and used metal detectors in the hope of finding further evidence or an additional murder weapon. Others carried out door-to-door enquiries. Croxford said nothing appeared to have been stolen and he admitted police were baffled. 'There was jewellery left on the television set in the house and about £20 in cash nearby,' he said. 'We have no idea why Mrs Davies was murdered.' In fact, there had also been about £1,800 in takings stashed in Ivy's 'safe' — the kitchen oven that she very rarely used.

The following day, detectives issued a vague description of a suspect. He was seen early on the morning of 4 February on the steps in nearby Seaforth Road, which ran parallel to Holland Road, heading towards the train station. The man was described as dark-haired, tall and in his 30s. 'We can't exclude the possibility that this person could strike again,' warned Mitchell. He also admitted police had no idea what Ivy was doing between locking up the café and the next morning, when her body was found. 'So far no-one seems to have seen her,' he told reporters. Croxford said a red or white wallet-type purse was missing from Ivy's home, but it was not known whether it contained any money.

On 9 February, detectives described two young people they wished to speak to. A young man and his girlfriend had been seen knocking on doors at guest houses and hotels in nearby Palmeira Avenue, despite having no luggage. The man was described as slim, between 5ft 10ins and 6ft and thin-faced with 'sharp features and collar-length greasy hair'. He was dressed in a Teddy-boy style jacket with red pocket flaps and dark trousers. Witnesses said he had a London accent and was aged between 28 and 30. The woman was said to be about 20 years old, with shoulder-length mousey hair. She was slim, medium build, about 5ft 4ins and wearing a dark coat. They were knocking on doors between 8.30pm and 9pm on the night Ivy was killed. Meanwhile, detectives were interviewing taxi drivers, workers at clubs, bars, bingo halls, cinemas and even the local dog track, in an effort to find out whether Ivy might have gone out that night.

Two days later, the 'Teddy boy' couple were identified and cleared.

Police continued to question anyone walking around the immediate area of the murder scene, but after nearly a month the search was becoming desperate. Detectives even made enquiries in Wales because of a hatchet attack on a 10-year-old girl near her home in Caerphilly, but the probe came to nothing. Ivy's ex-husband was also questioned.

By 1 March, detectives were ready to release more details about Ivy's murder. A small six-inch axe and a nine-inch knife, found in a garden in nearby Leigham Court Drive, Leigh-on-Sea, had been ruled out as possible murder weapons. Now, despite letting the local newspapers repeatedly tell their readers police were hunting a 'mad axeman', detectives revealed the pry bar found in a curtained alcove close to Ivy's body had caused the fatal injuries. The tool, typically used by mechanics or in a factory that uses gear wheels, was branded by the US-based tools company Snap-On and engraved '2050 USA'. One end was pointed while the other had an oval-shaped head with a sharp edge. It was twenty inches long, weighed about three pounds and was made of high tensile steel. Detectives believed it was fairly new. The tool had traces of Ivy's blood from where it had cracked her skull.

'This tool has come into our possession,' revealed Croxford. 'We are anxious to find its origin. We are making widespread enquiries among those who could have sold this type of tool.' Unknown to the general public, two men were questioned by officers. One, in his early 20s, provided an alibi. His friend made no comment in interview. Separately, a couple who lived nearby were also spoken to. 'We have got one or two lines to follow up,' Croxford said, enigmatically. Neither pair was ever charged. By this stage detectives were questioning men on building sites about the pry bar, as well as making enquiries with deckchair attendants on the beach and on Southend Pier.

By mid-March police had taken more than 460 statements and made more than 600 enquiries. Nothing seemed to stick.

Apparent sightings of Ivy during the night in question trickled in. Someone thought they had spotted her at the Queen's Hotel near her home in Westcliff. A woman matching her description was seen in a small lounge next to the cocktail bar at about 8pm. This 'Ivy' was wearing glasses, a white silk blouse with a roll-neck collar and a dark skirt. She appeared to be waiting for someone. Another witness said she saw Ivy at the Palace Bingo in Southend. The woman turned out to be Margaret Jewry, the mother of pop star Alvin Stardust. Margaret also ran a café, in the nearby town of Wickford, and wore glasses. She told the local paper it was a 'terrible coincidence'. The confusion may have arisen because Ivy and Margaret often played bingo together at the hotel.

Later that month, the *Evening Echo* ran a short piece about a mystery man wanted over the murder of a pensioner in the capital: 'The hunt for the murderer who preys on old women in West London was stepped up today. A senior detective warned: "He could be a sick man." The man has attacked 13 old women in the last four months. Widow Adele Price, 89, of Belgravia, was found strangled in her home on Monday night.'

Detectives in Southend had no reason to believe there was any link between the Ivy Davies case and the incidents in London. But the man who carried out the robberies and the killing of Adele Price would go on to become inextricably linked to their investigations.

On 20 March, police announced they were going to take fingerprints from 300 friends, family and associates of Ivy in what they called a 'dabs dragnet'. By now they had taken

900 statements. On 8 March, Croxford made an appeal on Anglia Television in which he issued a new e-fit of the suspect. The distinctive-looking man was described as 5ft 5ins, aged between 35 and 40, with greying sandy blond hair, brushed over to the right. He had a 'deep-lined face' with 'pointed features' and thick eyebrows. His fingers were nicotine-stained. Police said he was a regular at the Orange Tree but had not been seen there for a while.

A jury inquest took place on 7 April at the coroner's court in Southend. The pathologist, Dr Cameron, told how 'repeated blows with a heavy object, used with considerable force' had killed Ivy, leaving 'extensive and severe damage to her skull'. He gave the cause of death as cerebral contusion and said she was probably killed around midnight. Croxford told the coroner that his officers had interviewed a staggering 3,000 people across the county. They now believed Ivy stayed at home after locking up the Orange Tree. Sightings of the café owner out on the town could probably be attributed to Alvin Stardust's mother. After five minutes, a jury returned a verdict of murder, by person or persons unknown. Coroner Guy Jerman said: 'I now charge DCI Croxford with the responsibility of continuing these enquiries whether they take days, weeks or even years until someone or persons are brought to trial.'

Ivy was finally laid to rest at Southend's Sutton Road Cemetery on 17 April 1975. Her coffin carried the simple words: 'Ivy Lillian Davies, died February 4, 1975. 48 years, rest in peace.' Police mingled with the mourners, still suspecting that Ivy knew her killer. Her daughter Pat tearfully told the congregation: 'From now on this will be the family grave.' Ivy Junior's wreath said, 'Deepest love, miss you mum'. The local paper reported how Ivy's 18-year-old son, Victor, stood with his head bowed as fifty mourners followed the coffin to her grave.

A few weeks after Ivy was buried, customers at the still popular row of Westcliff cafés noticed a Black Maria — slang for a prisoner transfer van — pull up on the opposite side of the road, accompanied by two marked squad cars. A police presence in the area was no longer unusual following the exhaustive investigation, but this scenario was different.

Staff and diners peered curiously at the small convoy, but nobody got out the vehicles and nothing much happened. After a few minutes people turned their attention back to serving or eating their meals and the engines started up again. The Black Maria was accompanied up Shorefield Road, onto Station Road and then left onto Holland Road. The convoy made its way slowly down the street towards the empty shell of Ivy's once happy cottage, pausing for a few moments as it turned round.

Inside the van was a violent psychopath, fresh from confessing to the murders of two old women and a priest who he had hacked to death with an axe. Detectives were told the man had been bragging to fellow prisoners about the murder of Ivy Davies while on remand in Brixton Prison. But locked in the back of the van with Southend's finest, he now claimed he did not recognize the Orange Tree café or Ivy's cottage.

The man would never be convicted or charged with the crime. His name was Patrick David Mackay and police believed he was Britain's most prolific serial killer.

* * *

Fast forward forty-two years to early 2017 and there was still no sign of justice for Ivy Davies or her family. Victor Davies — who was just 18 years old when his mother was murdered — was actively campaigning for Essex Police to keep the investigation going, but he feared any potential suspect could now be dead or nearing the end of his life. As part of his efforts, he spoke to me on the phone one winter morning, fleshing out the parts of the story that had never been made public.

As we spoke, he paced up and down the garden because recalling his mother's murder always made him angry and anxious. At the end of our conversation Vic told me he had chain smoked at least half a pack of cigarettes.

As it turned out, Vic and Ivy had not been on particularly good terms when she died, and it soon became clear why. First, he wanted me to know it always upset him that people didn't know how many children she had. In order of age there was Patricia, Ivy Junior, Susan, Vic, David, Stephen and Carol. Another daughter, Karen, died aged three months. Ivy had been married to a soldier and most of the children were born at army bases around the country. Vic, for example, was born in Liverpool. But Ivy's husband physically and mentally abused her.

'She divorced my father and the reason was probably to do with abuse,' Vic said. 'I remember my father giving me a cup of tea to take to my mother once, but she wasn't in the bedroom, she was down the stairs in the cellar. I woke her up with this cup of tea and she was covered in bruises. These things stick in your mind. They never go away. That's probably why she put us in the home.'

It was a sorry tale. Vic said that after his parents divorced in about 1960, Ivy moved from where the family were living in Yorkshire to Westcliff. She met another soldier who was based in barracks at Shoeburyness, near Westcliff. He was later posted to Colchester, in the north of the county, and wanted to take Ivy with him. But there was a catch. He refused to raise another man's kids, let alone seven of them. So Ivy did what most mothers would never dream of doing, she gave all but her eldest two girls up.

'She put us in the Seaview Children's Home in Shoeburyness,' explained Vic. 'It's not there now. I ended up in a foster home but it was terrible. I was given a lot of abuse there. Physical abuse. Eventually they put me back in the home.' Vic acknowledged that Ivy wasn't quite the angelic figure she was made out to be following her death, even going so far as to call her 'cold'. Yet despite hardly knowing his mother for most of his life, he was refusing to give up on her. I wondered why.

When he was little more than a toddler, Vic explained, he and his siblings were allowed out of the children's home to walk west from Shoeburyness, along Southend seafront and to Westcliff. One time, he stopped at the forty-seven steps leading up to Holland Road and felt an instinctive urge to climb them. Ivy was back in the area, having only stayed with her new soldier for about eight months before returning to Westcliff. Although she had not been able to get her old house back, she had somewhat miraculously been able to lease a cottage in the very same street. Vic knocked on a door and luckily the woman who answered knew Ivy well.

'She looked down at me and said, "I know who you are,"' recalled Vic. 'The woman took me along to my mother's house and plonked me down. I remember her looking at me as if to say, "Now what am I going to do with you?"'

The meeting began a thaw in the frosty relations between Ivy, Vic and some, but not all, of her children. Vic believed Ivy had tried to get them all back when she returned from Colchester but she had, unsurprisingly given her willingness to abandon them just months earlier, been turned down by social services. Daughters Ivy Junior and Pat would later come to work for Ivy at the Orange Tree, but few of her friends knew about the other offspring, even amid the huge publicity following her death.

I asked Vic how he managed to forgive his mother. 'I understood it,' he replied. 'She probably feared violence if she didn't do as she was told. Not all of my brothers and sisters understood it but I did.'

Vic started visiting his mother every Thursday at 7pm. They would walk along Southend seafront and play games in the arcades or have dinner at an Italian restaurant in the high street. But Vic never moved into Ivy's home in Holland Road and, when he was older, he was forced to find his own digs.

'She was such a private person,' he said. 'She wouldn't open the door to anyone if it wasn't their time. You would just get a head out the window telling you to go away. After her murder, the newspaper reports said she was a bubbly person. She wasn't like that with her children, but I think she was trying to get to know us.'

By January 1974, Vic had found himself in serious trouble with the law. Having to fend for himself from a young age had led to a career in petty theft. That, in turn, led to a spell in borstal. When Vic decided borstal wasn't for him, he absconded. By January 1975, Vic was 18 years old and locked up in a tough young offenders' institution in Northampton and that was where Ivy wrote to him shortly before her death. 'It was a Dear John letter, basically,' he said. 'She was disgusted with me and told me she never wanted to see me again.' Sadly, her wish would come true.

Vic still recalls the day he found out about her murder with heart-breaking clarity:

> 'That week was my turn to be in charge of the television. It was about 5.45pm and the news was just starting. I think *The Monkees* was about to start on the other side and I was going to change the channel. Just then the headline said, "Murder in Southend". I said, "Hold on a minute, lads. I want to see if I know who it is." The next thing I know a picture of my mother is on the TV. I couldn't quite understand what was going on. I just stared. Someone said, "Do you know who it is then?" I was frozen.'

When Vic realized the full horror of what had happened to his mother, he spent two weeks recovering in the prison's hospital wing. Detectives arrived to question him. They revealed that prison bosses knew about Ivy's death prior to the television announcement but decided not to tell Vic because they assumed the pair were estranged after the Dear John letter. Vic said the decision was 'intentionally cruel'. To make matters worse, the police officers who came to the prison knew him from his wayward days in Southend and were automatically suspicious. 'They played the good cop, bad cop routine,' said Vic. 'They asked me if I knew anything about it. I know they were just doing their jobs but I couldn't believe it. I just said they should get out there and find out who killed my mum.'

After his release, Vic never committed another crime. 'What happened made me grow up a bit. I was never a master criminal and I have not been in trouble since. I decided to change.' As if Vic's story needed a tragic footnote, he revealed his father, by then a hospital porter, died in a car crash about ten years later in a head-on smash caused by an on-call doctor. But the purpose of Vic's phone call was really to tell me about a potential development in the case. The only previous breakthrough had come in 2005, when a 68-year-old man from Basildon — about sixteen miles down the A127 — was arrested on suspicion of Ivy's murder. He was later released without charge[*].

Now there was a tantalizing new lead. A former waitress from the Orange Tree had been in touch with him about an incident that happened in the café before Ivy's murder, as Vic explained:

> 'She told me about this time a doctor from Runwell Mental Hospital came into the café. He claimed he was leading a day out with patients from the hospital, but it later turned out that this "doctor" was a patient who had absconded and he was with a load of other runaways. Apparently, it all got covered up to save them embarrassment. None of

---

[*] This aspect of the case will be revisited in chapter nine, Unsolved.

it ever made the papers. My mum arranged to meet this man in town later that day, but I don't know if she did. I know he later turned up at her house. I'm not sure when it happened exactly, but he could be a suspect.'

After some toing and froing, the woman named him as Patrick Mackay. Vic was instantly sceptical. 'They wasted eight months looking into him,' he told me. 'I don't think he did it.' Nevertheless, Vic wanted to me to write a story about Mackay and his possible involvement because, even if the new lead was a red herring, he thought it would keep the story fresh in the minds of the public. He was concerned that with Mackay nudging his 70s and some of the other suspects now even older, time was running out to uncover the truth.

What follows is the story of Patrick Mackay, the crimes he committed and the several unsolved murders — including that of Ivy Davies — that led authorities to label him the most dangerous man in Britain.

Chapter 2

The Madness of Patrick Mackay

By the summer of 1975, answering questions about unsolved murders had become something of a hobby for Patrick Mackay. He had already admitted to the brutal axe murder of a Catholic priest, who was killed just two months after Ivy Davies. He had also confessed to three other killings and was now cooped up in jail awaiting a court date.

Mackay seemed to revel in telling fellow inmates he was even more dangerous than the police believed, by claiming to be responsible for other notorious unsolved crimes. Even the most thuggish members of HMP Brixton's population were understandably cautious around the wiry 22-year-old, who was 6ft 2ins tall and prone to uncontrollable fits of rage. Despite this, news of Mackay's prison-cell confessions soon made their way back to murder squads across London and the east of England, via criminals being held on remand who were looking to curry favour with the authorities. Consequently, Mackay was regularly taken out to police stations and crime scenes by detectives hoping to extract further confessions.

In an effort to work out who else he may have killed, the detectives dug into Mackay's past, including where he might have lived, worked and been incarcerated. It became increasingly complex, with a seemingly endless number of periods spent in psychiatric hospitals or jail. At the same time, Mackay began writing a prison memoir, primarily for use in his defence case, in which he detailed some of the more dramatic and tragic aspects of his youth. He also agreed to release his medical records to journalists in a bid to improve his chances of being sent to a psychiatric hospital for treatment rather than prison.

Every available source painted a picture of a deeply troubled young man, whose problems were rooted in a violent family home and a dysfunctional relationship with his alcoholic father, Harold Murray Mackay. Ironically, the father of the boy who would grow up to become one of Britain's most violent killers was the son of an upstanding but grizzled detective inspector in the Glasgow City Police. On the surface, Harold, like his father, was also a model citizen. Polite, quiet and introverted, he had a softly spoken voice and his Scottish lilt and gentle tone would be passed on to his son, Patrick. Professionally, Harold aspired to be an accountant.

However, with the outbreak of the Second World War, Harold had no hesitation in joining up to fight for his country against the Nazis. Within months he was embroiled in fierce fighting with the Eighth Army, also known as the Desert Rats, in North Africa. Much of it took place in the deserts of Egypt and Libya, initially in response to Italy entering the war. But when Rommel's German Afrika Corps joined the fray the fighting intensified. The Eighth Army famously took part in the decisive battles of El-Alamein, in July, October and November 1942, but by then the young Harold Mackay had already been seriously injured.

Lance Corporal Mackay was on a routine patrol near Alexandria in 1941 when he heard a bullet whistle past his head and the sharp crack of rifle fire a millisecond later. His squad was under heavy attack. Another bullet tore through his forearm, leaving blood gushing from a deep wound. Harold hit the deck and as he lay there — convinced that these moments were his last — his comrades fell around him, one after another. He was the only survivor of the ambush; a harsh fact that tortured him until the day he died.

As well as the bitter experience of watching his friends die, Harold also carried with him a physical reminder of his service. As a result of his injuries he had a metal plate inserted into his right arm, which continued to cause him pain and discomfort long after the visceral realities of the fighting ended. He rarely spoke about his memories of the war to anyone other than his son, Patrick. Many years after the conflict, he would sit the lad on his knee and regale him with horrific tales of death and destruction from the North African campaign. But before Patrick came along, Harold would experience another tragedy.

After the war, the shy and unassuming Harold had settled into his dream job as an accountant. By 1947 he was married and there was a baby on the way but both his wife and infant died during childbirth. The worst horrors of war seemed like nothing compared with this fresh, unfathomably cruel turn of events. Harold was plunged into a whirlpool of despair and he began to block out the pain with copious amounts of whisky.

Three years later and still devastated by the loss, Harold set his sights on leaving the country and signed up for a three-year job on a sugar plantation in British Guiana, South America, working as a bookkeeper. His luck took a turn for the better when he met a 36-year-old Creole woman named Marion Eloise McWatt. Romance blossomed and Marion was pregnant with his child when the pair married in February 1952. But by marrying, Harold had broken his contract with the plantation company and he was forced to return to London. Marion joined him four months later.

He was now back working as an accountant, but by this time he was a full-blown alcoholic. Whether the cause was his problem drinking, his memories of the war, the death of his first wife and child or resentment at having lost his new job for the love of a woman, he began to physically punish those around him, especially his wife. On one occasion, he kicked the pregnant Marion in the stomach, yet, despite his violence, Marion gave birth to a baby boy on 25 September 1952, at the Park Royal Hospital in Middlesex. The couple named him Patrick David.

Younger sisters Ruth and Heather arrived in 1954 and 1957 and the family lived, apparently happily, in Kensal Rise, North London. But Harold continued to beat his wife and the violence soon extended to Patrick. However, the youngster seemed to find his father's attacks instructional and when he started school he established himself as a playground thug. When the family moved to Dartford in Kent, Patrick became the leading bully at St Alban's Road Infants' School. He was big for his age and exploited his size by picking on younger children, especially girls, including his sister Ruth. He hung around in a gang of mostly younger boys and would steal, tell lies and make little effort in classes — except art, a subject that would become a life-long passion.

Roland Hayes was a school friend. In 2012, he told makers of the documentary *Born to Kill: The Devil's Disciple* about his memories of Mackay and the bizarre behaviour he exhibited even then:

> 'In the playground, we was [sic] all like young animals running around. Some good people, some bad people, and Patrick Mackay was one of the bad people. He was in a special class, what would be called special needs children these days, but in those days they were just trouble. He was like a little terrorist. There would be a girl there talking to a friend and he would come running in from a side he couldn't be seen from, blindsiding her, and he would shove her or pinch her or push her and run off again. The girl would be crying. He would be looking over his shoulder, laughing, running off and planning his next move.

'After school we used to go walking around the
town a little bit and we used to go exploring. We
used to climb up this verge through the trees, then
to some wasteland and we used to play around up
there. The first time I went up there with Patrick
Mackay he picked a bell-shaped flower, filled it up
with his urine and drunk it in front of me. I was
absolutely gobsmacked, which was the reason he
did it. It was just to shock me. He seemed to have a
split personality. You could talk to him, he seemed
to be normal enough, but then he would run off on
these long legs and snatch something off of a pub
table and run off with it or something. Or run into
the front of a shop, snatch something and run off
again. Then he would come back with me and then
he would be normal again.'

Throughout Patrick's schooldays, his father Harold continued
to drink heavily and a grim routine set in. He would arrive home
from work, frustrated and stinking of booze. Then, as a matter
of habit, he would attack his family. Marion bore the brunt of
his rages, but all three children would watch. Exactly what took
place and what kind of trauma this inflicted on the youngsters
will never be known. But Mackay gave some insight into the
violence in his prison memoir: 'Up until his death my father
used to get violently drunk, shout, scream and always when he
was like this beat me with the back of his hand and sometimes
his fist,' he wrote. 'He must have had a tremendous drinking
problem, but of course he would never say so. I remember that
my father never at all hit my two sisters when drunk, but only
me and my mother. He would make a lot of filthy accusations
towards her. This would take place usually Friday nights and
Saturday nights. It was plain bloody regular.'

To compound the misery, Harold also cut back on household
spending, principally to fund his alcoholism. This meant the

family could go weeks without hot water and the three Mackay children would be packed off to school in dirty, smelly clothes. Patrick would beg neighbours to use their baths and teachers raised concerns about the state of the children's underwear. Unsurprisingly, Patrick hated school and the home life created by his booze-addled father. He felt starved of affection and the only genuine intimacy with Harold came when he listened to the old man's gory tales from the war. Patrick seemed to enjoy these sessions and became fascinated not just with the war, but with death itself. As he got older this interest manifested, itself as a twisted devotion to Nazi ideology.

In 1961, Harold Mackay finally sought refuge in a psychiatric hospital and begged for help with his drinking. He was admitted to Langley Green Hospital near Epsom, Surrey, which treated people with acute mental health problems, and then became an inpatient at Stone House Hospital, formerly the City of London Lunatic Asylum, near his home in Dartford. Years later, Patrick would become a regular at Stone House.

But just a year after Harold sought treatment for his drinking, he was back on the whisky. For Marion Mackay and her family, the abuse only came to an end on 8 November 1962 when Harold left for work as normal. Pausing before he closed the door behind him, his last words to his son were, 'Remember to be good.' That morning, Harold suffered a heart attack at Holborn Viaduct Station and died soon afterwards at St Bartholomew's Hospital in the City of London. He was 42 years old.

Harold's short life had been unhappy: marred by the horrors of war, the death of the woman he loved and his unborn child, and battles with alcohol and mental health problems. In return, he had made those around him unhappy with his violent and abusive behaviour. He was repatriated to his native Scotland and Patrick neither viewed his body nor attended the funeral.

Medical reports would later reveal how Harold's death had a long-standing effect on Patrick. Initially, when the boy heard the news from a neighbour on the way home from school, he said very little and became withdrawn. As time went on, he refused to accept the reality of his father's death and would repeatedly ask his mother when his dad was coming home. Throughout his life, Mackay would tell people his father was still alive and that he could hear his voice. Perhaps the youngster felt, bizarrely considering Harold's despicable behaviour, that he had lost his moral compass. Harold, a staunch Catholic, had forced his family to attend church and Patrick was steeped in the ways of Christian ideas of good and evil, and the Ten Commandments — particularly 'Honour your father and mother.' Yet with Harold gone, Patrick would viciously and repeatedly break this and other commandments, including, most notably, 'Thou shalt not kill.'

In his memoir, Mackay remarked on the effect his father's death had on him: 'I ceased to be just a naughty boy and became a delinquent. I seemed to change within myself to an extreme extent all round.'

With his father dead, Patrick decided at the age of 10, that he was now the man of the house. He would throw violent tantrums if someone tried to stop him sitting in his father's chair. He became convinced his mother favoured his sisters and would fly into rages, sometimes appearing to have fits where he would froth at the mouth. Within a year, Marion was in hospital, suffering from a nervous breakdown. She stayed there for four months. Patrick was shunted into a foster home in the Herne Bay area of Kent, where his tantrums grew even worse. The boy was unable to grasp why his father, and now his mother, had abandoned him.

When the family was reunited in early 1964, his behaviour became even more chilling. Like many serial killers, the young Patrick Mackay took to torturing and killing animals, even playing with their corpses as if they were toys. He attacked his pet dog, his rabbit and a neighbour's cat. He was often seen by neighbours playing with dead birds in the garden, throwing them up in the air and catching them. In one particularly nasty episode, Patrick killed his family's pet tortoise by roasting it over an open fire. He threw the corpse into a neighbour's garden. The youngster would also ask morbid questions about the state of his father's decomposing body. He was keenly interested in death and violence and, when he felt lonely, would console himself with memories of his father's tales about the bloody conflict in Africa. He also thirsted to find out more about Harold's wartime opponents — the Nazis.

He continued to pick on younger children, developing a reputation as a bully not just at school but in the wider area of Gravesend. He savoured the notoriety. On one occasion, he threatened a grown woman with a pitchfork. He would set fire to beach huts for entertainment and took to stealing hens and garden gnomes from his neighbours.

In June 1964 Patrick carried out what would be the first of many crimes against God by setting fire to a curtain in a Catholic church. For some reason, perhaps because of his father's insistence on going to church, he harboured a lifelong grudge against institutional religion, even though during his life he became close friends with two priests.

A month after the church blaze, 11-year-old Patrick Mackay made his first appearance in court, charged with twenty-one offences, including the fire, the theft of the hens, some garden gnomes and a small amount of cash. Dartford Juvenile Court remanded him for fourteen days and he was released later that month, having been sentenced to three years' probation. Neighbours begged the authorities to remove him from the area, but their pleas went unheeded.

By the end of 1964, Patrick had grown into a well-built youth on the verge of his teens and his violent rages became increasingly dangerous, both for those around him and for himself. Police were called to the family home up to four times a week as he smashed the place up or barricaded himself inside. He rarely attended school, and on one occasion he attacked a policewoman, Amy Tapp, when she tried to stop him playing truant. 'He was just like a caged animal,' she would say later. 'He was emotionally very disturbed and at the time very mental. I felt that he should be put somewhere, shut away, so that nobody could be damaged as a result of his mental reaction to people. He was violent and obviously would hurt somebody in the end.'

* * *

Between the ages of 12 and 22, Patrick was 'shut away' on nineteen separate occasions, either in psychiatric hospitals, special schools or prison. However, none of his spells off the streets lasted very long. His first encounter with mental health professionals came when a psychiatrist paid him a home visit following a violent tantrum. Patrick was given an electro-encephalogram (EEG), which monitored his brainwaves. They were found to be normal, although the psychiatrist thought the young man should be removed from the family home for everyone's wellbeing.

Meanwhile, because he refused to meet with his probation officer, steps were underway to change the probation order made at the juvenile court for the arson attack and string of petty crimes. Magistrates replaced it with a 'fit person order', which meant he was deemed not fit to live at home with his family. In a traumatic upheaval for the troubled young man, he was sent to Glebelands, a home for disturbed children, at Harrietsham near Maidstone. While there he attended Pinewood School, but he was typically disruptive.

Rather than feeling relief that somebody was at last trying to control her unpredictable son, Marion was dismayed. She applied to overturn the order and Patrick came home to Gravesend just before Christmas 1965. But it wasn't long before he was back in another institution.

On 6 January 1966, he attacked his mother and two sisters and was admitted to West Hill General Hospital in Dartford, but was released two weeks later. A consultant psychiatrist, Dr James Willis, wrote that he believed his father, the cruel Harold, was a psychopath who had passed on the trait genetically to his son. It was the first of several occasions when the label of psychopath would be applied to Patrick Mackay.

Despite clinical fears that Patrick might be a psychopath, the definition of the term was fairly loose in the late 1960s and early 1970s, and it was far from clear how the condition should be treated. The first edition of the American Psychiatric Association's *Diagnostic and Statistical Manual of Mental Disorders* (*DSM*) published in 1952, used the term 'sociopathic personality disturbance'. It listed four subtypes: antisocial, dyssocial, sexual and addictive. The antisocial subtype included people who are 'chronically in trouble and do not seem to change as a result of experience or punishment, with no loyalties to anyone.' It noted that this personality type typically displayed callousness, a lack of responsibility and the ability to rationalize awful behaviour. The definition seemed to fit Mackay like a glove. But then the 'dyssocial' label also seemed to apply to him as this was for people who 'disregard societal rules, although they are capable of strong loyalties to others or groups.' Patrick definitely ignored the rules, but he was apparently loyal to his deceased father and was certainly capable of making friends.

The second edition, *DSM-II*, published in 1968, refined the definitions and did away with the dyssocial subtype, instead focusing on the 'antisocial personality' and its incapacity for loyalty, a preponderance towards selfishness, irresponsibility and lack of empathy. The eminent psychologist Ronald Blackburn would later write that psychopathy was an 'infinitely elastic, catch-all category' and would complain that doctors were often forced into making a moral judgment about patients instead of a clinical diagnosis.

Meanwhile, British psychiatrists also had to bear in mind the strictures of the Mental Health Act, 1959. The category of 'psychopathic personality' had been added to new legislation and covered anyone who had a 'persistent disorder or disability of mind which results in abnormally aggressive or seriously irresponsible conduct.' It meant that anyone diagnosed as a psychopath could only be treated voluntarily, or within a strict legal framework. Whereas in the past Patrick Mackay might have been locked away in a lunatic asylum indefinitely, the pressure was now on to release him from the moment he was admitted to any mental institution.

The researcher Bob Hare developed a 'psychopath checklist' in the late 1970s as a result of working with prisoners in Canadian jails. Today, the Hare Psychopathy Checklist is used by psychiatrists the world over and is generally accepted as providing a solid diagnosis of psychopathy. It has twenty key points and scoring highly in the test — as long as it is administered by a clinical professional — probably means the subject is a psychopath. Signifiers include superficial charm, a grandiose sense of self-worth, manipulativeness, lack of empathy, criminal versatility, impulsiveness, irresponsibility, poor behavioural controls and juvenile delinquency. Psychopaths are also usually fascinated by death.

This all fitted the young Patrick Mackay perfectly. The trouble was that when the death-obsessed delinquent first started coming in to contact with psychiatrists, there was no Bob Hare checklist and no universally acknowledged definition of his condition. As a result, when Marion was told her son was probably a psychopath, it meant nothing to her. In her eyes, he was simply a very naughty boy still struggling to come to terms with his father's death.

Shortly after being released from his first spell in hospital, Mackay attacked his sister again and was re-admitted. Doctors wrote to nearby psychiatric hospitals about the now 13-year-old's 'uncontrollable rage', begging them to take him in as a patient. But Patrick was returned home to his family. Another domestic incident occurred soon after and he was hauled back before the courts. This time, a second fit person order was made and he was taken to Beech House, the juvenile wing of St Augustine's Hospital near Canterbury.

Patrick felt like a caged animal at Beech House and absconded almost on a weekly basis. Doctors noted his 'infantile' behaviour, which included taking a doll to bed with him each evening and insisting everyone kiss it goodnight. On a darker note, he would often talk about wanting to die and would use foul language when discussing his sisters.

In June 1966 Patrick appeared in court for a second time, on this occasion charged with the theft of a bicycle trailer. He was given a twelve-month conditional discharge and ordered back to Beech House. However, when, after a few days, he absconded again, the hospital made the decision to discharge him. Patrick had made it clear he had no wish to be treated there and doctors decided that having to track him down after his multiple vanishing acts was more trouble than it was worth.

Magistrates decided to send him to Court Lees Approved School near Redhill in Surrey. The school catered for about 160 boys of secondary school age, mostly offenders. The school routine was highly regimented and its attendees were subject to the discipline lacking in their everyday lives. But the practices there were also open to abuse.

Patrick worked on the school's farm and played sports, but he didn't take well to the rules and would rather be practising his art. Art would be a passion for him throughout his life, including during his long periods of incarceration. He was handed corporal punishment on a regular basis and was brutally caned for absconding during a home visit in October 1966. It was during another home visit in January the following year that Patrick saw an extreme way out of the school — he tried to gas himself by sticking his head in the oven. This landed him back in the psychiatric wing of West Hill Hospital, in Dartford. However, despite pleas from doctors and his mother, Patrick was sent back to Court Lees school, although he eventually returned home. Soon afterwards, the school hit the headlines.

An anonymous letter published in *The Guardian* in March 1967 detailed the 'savage use of the cane' and the horrific bruising left on boys' backsides after they were punished for absconding. Photos of the boys' bruised buttocks were sent to the *Daily Mail* and were later published to great uproar in *The Times*. An editorial in the *Mail* pointed out that far from reforming the boys, the severity of the treatment was likely to make them more hardened criminals. Ivan Cook, a master at the school, wrote prophetically in *The Observer* about Mackay, although he didn't name him. He said, 'I know of a boy, free at the moment, of whom a psychiatrist wrote: "He is a potential murderer of women."'

When an enquiry was carried out by leading lawyer E.B. Gibbens, he wrote specifically about the trauma absconders such as Patrick endured at Court Lees: 'Boys brought back to the school after absconding...are caned forthwith upon their return, whatever the hour. Thus it often happens that a boy who arrives at the school late at night disconsolate, tired after a long journey and probably emotionally upset, is immediately caned. Any preliminary enquiry by the headmaster as to the reason for the absconding is probably cursory.'

There is no way of knowing just how often Patrick was abused in this way, but the type of punishment meted out to boys was deemed sufficient for it to be closed down later that year, eventually followed by the entire approved school system. Yet it was too late for Patrick Mackay. Already prone to acts of criminality, he was soon to become one of the estimated sixty per cent of pupils who went on to re-offend. And he would do so over and over again.

With Patrick free from Court Lees, Marion took her family to her native British Guiana. The move was intended to be permanent, but it was soon aborted after relatives became tired of Patrick's violent moods. The family's swift return to England brought him into closer contact with Marion's sisters,

Christina and Ruby, because the family was forced to move into the sisters' flat in Jessica Road, Wandsworth. The cramped conditions led to simmering tensions and it didn't take long for Patrick to lash out physically at his mother. Once again, he was forced to attend a school for juvenile delinquents, this time the Classifying School in Redhill. He spent three months there, during which time it was discovered that his forced committal was illegal because the approved school order had been discharged to allow the family to move to South America. Eventually, Patrick made his way back to his mother's new home in Frobisher Way, Gravesend. It was a move that years later would have devastating repercussions for a nearby priest, Father Anthony Crean.

The relocation back to Kent marked a dramatic deterioration in Patrick's behaviour. Taking a succession of low-paid and ultimately unsuccessful jobs, the teenager would roam the area and travel into London looking for work and visiting his aunts. On one occasion, he attacked two young boys on a building site, smashing their heads into the ground. He was charged with violent assault. On 17 March 1968, Patrick attacked his mother in the family home, throwing her and his sisters out of the house. He only allowed them back inside after the police arrived and calmed the situation down. But two months later, he tried to strangle his mother. He then tried to gas himself and stab himself with a bayonet. It was his most violent breakdown yet.

Patrick was detained under the Mental Health Act and admitted to Stone House Hospital, with a note from Dr Gerald Ellis which said he was a 'source of danger to himself and his family'. The hospital had treated his father shortly before his death. He was assessed by Dr James Stewart, who found Patrick problematic but not suffering from delusions (although he had told police he still lived in Dartford with his father). However, Dr Stewart noted that 'when angry he might easily become confused and afterwards be amnesiac.' Despite this, he was allowed home four days later.

Two days after his release, Patrick appeared at Wandsworth Juvenile Court for the assault on the two boys. He was, once again, handed two years' probation and ordered to undergo non-specified 'treatment', which never took place. Three weeks later, he launched another attack on his mother. He was seen again by Dr Ellis and detained at Stone House for another seventy-two-hour observation period. 'He remembers being upset but does not give any clear account of what happened,' wrote the doctor. 'He is creating a major problem in the home by his behaviour and actions. I am sure that this is entirely a personality disorder, but he is also subject to fits of depression and very often is maniacal in his rage.' Patrick later explained that he had become angry at the sight of one of his sisters and her friend watching the television. He was released a few days later.

On 26 July 1968, Patrick again attacked a stranger in the street when he tried to strangle a young boy near his Dartford home. He also stole the boy's watch, but threw it away. He would go on to repeat this pattern in other crimes. He was arrested and taken to the Ashford Remand Centre for Juveniles. There he was seen by Dr Christopher Fysh and a psychiatrist, Dr Leonard Carr. For the first time, Patrick's history of violent outbursts was researched and a proper diagnosis reached.

Dr Carr's analysis of the troubled 15 year old was stark. Patrick had an 'explosive temper' and without intervention would go on to become a 'cold psychopathic killer', wrote the doctor. He implored the Essex Assizes to commit him to a psychiatric hospital. After being found guilty of the assault, Patrick was indeed sent to the secure Moss Side Hospital, in Maghull, near Liverpool. The date was 17 October 1968.

Patrick Mackay would later bemoan his time at Moss Side, stating that he was not correctly diagnosed. 'In Moss Side I was classified as a psychopath but without mania,' he said. 'I have always believed that I have not just the problem of being psychopathic on its own, but instead having psychopathic mania. This has always been my personal opinion on the matter, and believe no-one [can] judge one's mind better in most cases than oneself. Since the mind is such a complex machine.'

Moss Side was overcrowded and security was tight. For Patrick, it was yet another deprivation of his liberty after the Court Lees school, the Classifying School, the remand centres and Stone House.

He later complained about not being able to take his O-Levels. He also believed that advice given to him about his temper was insufficient because he was told to simply walk away when he felt himself becoming angry. Patrick, perhaps correctly, felt it was impossible for him to do so because of the compulsive element — or the 'mania' — inherent in his psychopathy.

After three months, he and a group of other patients formulated a plan to attack a nurse and escape, but they were foiled before it could come to fruition. It was a sign of his growing frustration. Marion visited him regularly and believed he had reformed, unaware that psychopaths cannot simply decide to be better people. Perhaps she felt he had heeded her late husband's final piece of advice — 'Remember to be good.'

Marion began calling for Patrick's release and writing to the Liverpool Mental Health Review Tribunal. The doctors opposed her and in October 1969 the order was renewed. Undeterred, she appealed to the tribunal again on 14 November. The hospital's deputy medical superintendent, Dr Robert Porter, pleaded with the lay board not to release him.

'He suffers from psychopathic disorder,' he said. 'He is immature, lacking in judgment, insight and social responsibility. He has been convicted of arson, assault occasioning actual bodily harm, robbery with violence, store breaking and larceny. He would not remain voluntarily in any hospital or other establishment. The responsible medical officer considers that the patient continues to need detention for medical treatment and is not at present fit for discharge from hospital.'

Patrick remained quiet and polite throughout the hearing. He charmed the tribunal, as psychopaths are known to do, and was released on 4 December 1969.

After failing to keep two low-paid jobs secured for him by his probation officer, Patrick resumed the violent attacks on his mother. Eventually Marion kicked him out and he went to live with his aunts in Wandsworth, much against their wishes. He found a job with the Kensington and Chelsea Borough Council, working as a gardener's labourer, but the violence continued. On one occasion, he wrapped his hands around Aunt Christina's throat, warning that he could choke her, before releasing his grip. As a result, he moved into a hostel for a week before hitch-hiking back to Gravesend.

In July 1970 Patrick suffered another major episode, again attacking his mother. His probation officer, Bernard Fleming, arrived at the house and described Patrick as being 'agitated' and talking 'wildly' about 'detesting everyone, including the world'.

'He looked at his hand and said that even seeing a part of himself made him sick,' explained Fleming. 'I noted that he had a number of photographs and models of Nazis in his bedroom. He broke a toy rifle rack whilst I was talking to him and said that he could do what he liked with his own property. He frequently clenched his fists and his anger burst out in expressions of hate for his mother and all women. He said that he should not have been born, and that wherever he was, trouble soon found him. He said that he would smash his bedroom window and cut his wrist, but he made no attempt.'

Patrick was eventually sent back to Stone House under a twenty-eight-day observation order. It was his fourth stay in a psychiatric hospital in two years. A few days later — after winning back his civilian clothes as a reward for good behaviour — he absconded. Marion welcomed him back home. A week later, he attacked her once more, twisting her arm behind her back. He barricaded himself in his room and jammed a bayonet between the door and his chest, in the hope that anyone coming in would drive it into him. He was returned to Stone House once again. There he was told that an order had been made under Section 26 of the Mental Health Act requiring him to remain in the hospital and receive treatment for up to one year. He flew into a rage and immediately absconded but was captured and returned to the hospital. He ran amok, climbing onto the roof and attacking a fireman who tried to bring him down.

It was about this time that Patrick announced he wanted to be known by a memorable new name: Franklin Bolvolt the First. He said it was a 'name to be feared and remembered, like Hitler's' and it would be a catalyst for world-wide change under his leadership. It was the clearest sign yet that he was an untreatable psychopath with dangerous leanings towards megalomania.

On 28 August 1970, he was transferred back to the more secure Moss Side Hospital. He wrote to his mother regularly, promising to behave and learn a trade. In return, Marion applied for Patrick's release to the tribunal three times, in December 1970, June 1971 and January 1972, but all three appeals were turned down. She tried again in July 1972. To the dismay of doctors, this time the tribunal granted her wish. Patrick Mackay was a free man once more. It was a decision that would go on to wreck dozens of lives.

Patrick Mackay was now an adult, and he returned to Gravesend where he immediately settled into his old routine of violent outbursts. But now, instead of being committed after each incident, he moved out for short periods of time.

While living at his aunt's flat in Wandsworth three years earlier, Mackay had made friends with the Cowdrey family — mum and dad Vi and Bert, teenage sons Denis, Terry and Leigh, and two younger daughters. They lived in a terraced house in Grantham Road, Stockwell, South London. Patrick often referred to Vi and Bert as 'mother' and 'father' and they indulged his drunken behaviour, allowing him to stay for one or several days at a time.

By this time, his sister Ruth was also being treated at Stone House for mental health problems and Patrick felt guilty about her illness, fearing he had brought it on. In February 1973, after another domestic incident, he readmitted himself voluntarily to Stone House although, as usual, he absconded and returned home.

He spent an increasing amount of time in London. The Cowdreys, his regular hosts, knew little of his medical history, let alone that he was a diagnosed psychopath. However, his violent side was becoming apparent. One night, after Patrick threatened to kill Vi during an outburst, she replied, 'If you think you're big enough you can try it,' and pushed him onto the settee. Luckily for her, he did not retaliate.

Patrick's interest in Nazism and fascism grew. He would praise Hitler and goosestep outside the Cowdreys' home, causing the family considerable embarrassment. He stole books about the Nazis from libraries and talked about their twisted ideas on genetics, euthanasia and the Holocaust in glowing terms. Despite his own mixed blood — which was of great concern to him — he fashioned his own Nazi uniform and built up a collection of Nazi memorabilia, including an Iron Cross which he kept around his neck, jackboots, and a two-foot wooden eagle and swastika. He spoke admiringly of Nero, Genghis Khan and Enoch Powell. At his mother's home in Gravesend, his bedroom was transformed into a Nazi shrine, with a picture of Himmler by his bed. 'If I ruled I'd exterminate all the useless old people,' he would boast.

Like the Nazis, Patrick Mackay had developed a warped sense of his own importance and an obsession with death. There was little doubt in his own mind that he was going to kill. He had already tried to strangle the boy in the street and his own mother, and he had briefly choked his aunt. The next stage of his criminal career would see him graduate from random acts of violence to a targeted campaign of burglary and, ultimately, cold-blooded murder.

Chapter 3

A Saint Valentine's Day Murder

While the decision to release Patrick Mackay from Moss Side would soon prove disastrous, there had been some early signs that he might have been able to live on the straight and narrow. He certainly wanted to earn money and took a succession of low-paid menial jobs to help contribute at home.

But Mackay had spent almost three years incarcerated alongside seriously unwell individuals and career criminals. He would later tell doctors about mixing with murderers at the secure hospital and enjoying their company. Whether or not his fellow inmates had a direct effect on his subsequent actions is unknown, but one thing is for sure, Mackay's long spell in Moss Side did absolutely nothing to curb his increasingly dangerous and violent behaviour.

Hospital doctors had assessed him as having a just below average IQ of ninety-two. He would often complain that he had been prevented from taking his O-Levels and as a result, this limited his employment prospects. Now, having obtained his freedom, Mackay became the classic itinerant worker, struggling to carry out the simplest of tasks and usually giving up after a few days or weeks. He had sixteen jobs between 1968 and his final arrest in 1975; a jam packed but unimpressive CV*.

As a psychopath burdened with a 'grandiose sense of self-worth' Mackay's inflated ego was partly behind his frequent decisions to quit. After all, he firmly believed he was destined for world domination under his alter ego Franklin Bolvolt the First. But alcohol and drug abuse also played a part. Nobody

---

* Mackay's work history paints a picture of a young man who was hopelessly restless and going nowhere. His first job was with an egg-packing firm in Battersea, south-west London, where he worked for three days after leaving school. In May 1968, he joined mineral water supplier Moore Brothers of Swanscombe, Kent, as a van boy. It is not known exactly when he left but a short time later he found himself doing his first stint in Moss Side. After his final release from the psychiatric hospital in October 1972, he worked as a park keeper for Gravesend Council for about a month. He also found occasional work as a labourer.

Between 26 February and 9 March 1973, he worked as a cutter serviceman at Imperial Paper Mills in Gravesend, but he only showed up twice until a manager sacked him saying he was a 'waste of time' with a 'split personality'. He went back to his job as a grass cutter with Gravesend Council on March 13 1973, but was let go after three days for being 'unreliable'. He then landed a job as an assistant caretaker at Southfields School on 3 April, but by the end of the month he'd quit.

Between 20 May and 22 June 1973, he worked as a road sweeper for Lambeth Council, again leaving of his own accord. He spent four days working as a cellar assistant with Reiniers the wine merchants, in Tachbrook Street, Pimlico, south-west London, between 2 July and 6 July but resigned after telling his boss he had been left a 'legacy'.

Mackay was jobless until 30 October 1973, before working as a van boy for Perrings Furniture, based in Woodhouse Road, Finchley. He quit on 5 January 1974. On 14 January, he started work as a labourer at the Tudor Sports Ground in Barnet, but stayed for just eleven days.

Between 4 March and 9 July, he found a job as a 'patrolling trustee' at Monken Hadley Common in Barnet. He then spent several months out of work, largely because of a prison sentence, before being employed as a gardener at St Pancras Cemetery in Islington on 3 December 1974. He left on 2 January 1975 and later that month landed another job as a gardener at East Finchley Cemetery, although he rarely turned up and was sacked on 7 February.

He also worked intermittently at the Chicken Inn, Leicester Square, and at Barnan's Packaging in Carlton Street, in the St James area.

likes working on a hangover, and more often than not Mackay's head was pounding due to the previous day's chemical overload. Like his father, he used alcohol to self-medicate. It gave him respite from his own tortured thoughts and might have helped stifle the unhappy memories of his time in Moss Side. Yet this abuse prevented him from developing a successful working life and most of his pay went on drink and drugs.

Amphetamine, or speed as it was known, was Mackay's drug of choice, along with copious amounts of whisky, usually glugged straight from the bottle. The speed craze had started in London in the 1960s and was an integral part of the Mod scene. Commonly taken as pills, known as purple hearts, possession became a criminal offence in 1964 but that only ensured its continuing popularity. By the time Mackay first tried the drug it was being snorted as a powder by followers of the Northern Soul and punk scenes, who themselves took many of their cultural reference points from the Mods.

Mackay didn't really belong to any popular youth scene, despite enjoying drugs and spending much of his time idling in pubs. It's hard to make friends when you have a penchant for extreme violence and your last permanent residence was a psychiatric hospital. His psychopathic personality didn't help; he had no real interest in other people and as a result most found him cold, aloof and uncomfortable to be around.

If Mackay had been asked to align himself to any social movement it would have been the fascist far right. It was probably coincidental, but amphetamines were popular in Nazi Germany as frontline troops necked chemical stimulants while cutting a swathe across Europe. Perhaps Mackay took the drug to spur him on in a quest to satisfy his own thirst for violence.

By early 1973 Mackay was enjoying his freewheeling lifestyle between London and Kent so much that he vowed he would never be locked up again. There was just one problem; he was a remorseless psychopath who had no control over his impulses.

His short-lived job as an assistant caretaker in Gravesend was a prime example. He stopped turning up after just three weeks, deciding instead to start committing burglaries. These crimes were usually of the walk-in variety at commercial premises, involving no violence, and often he merely stole food or a bottle of spirits. But on one occasion, during a spell of unemployment, fed up, bored and looking for a victim for his violent urges, he paid a visit to his mother's house and tried to strangle the family dog.

In May 1973, Mackay made a new friend. While roaming woodland near Shorne in Kent, he met Father Anthony Crean, the 63-year-old chaplain of the village convent. The pair spent the afternoon in one of Shorne's three pubs, the Rose and Crown, drinking whisky and smoking cigarettes. Mackay would often get through an entire wage packet in a single day in a London boozer, trying to buy the friendship of strangers by splashing out on round after round. But this time Father Crean seemed to enjoy buying the drinks. The pair began to meet regularly.

Yet just a few weeks later, Mackay broke into Father Crean's cottage and stole a cheque for £30. Crudely altering the handwriting, he cashed it in for £80 at a local bank. Father Crean reported the theft, but when Mackay was arrested the priest unsuccessfully asked for the charges to be dropped. Mackay appeared at Northfleet Magistrates' Court in Kent on 21 June 1973, where he was fined £20 and given a two-year conditional discharge. He was also ordered to pay back the £80 to Father Crean. The pair briefly rekindled their friendship after Mackay vowed to comply with the court order, but predictably he didn't keep to his word. They fell out and Mackay went back to splitting his time between his mum's place in Kent, visiting the Cowdreys, and staying with his aunts at their new home in Montacute Road, Catford, in south-east London.

In March 1975, Mackay would return to Shorne to hack Father Crean to death with a knife and an axe. But before doing so, he honed his criminal skills on the streets of London.

Around the time he met Father Crean, Mackay was drinking up to ten pints of lager a day, plus at least half a bottle of Johnnie Walker Red Label — his whisky of choice — or vodka. Whether he was at the Cowdreys in Stockwell, his aunts' house in Catford or at his mother's in Gravesend, trouble — as he liked to say — always found him.

Father Crean was not his only ecclesiastical friend. Early in July 1973, Mackay contacted an Anglican curate, Reverend Edward 'Ted' Brack, who he knew from Gravesend and who now lived in Finchley, North London. The 36-year-old was working at the nearby St Barnabas Church, where he would remain until 1977, having survived at least one close call with the serial killer. He later became a team vicar at the St John on Bethnal Green Church, in East London, lodging with his heavy-drinking brother, John, in an adjoining property. He is fondly remembered today by parishioners, who recall his booming voice and his appreciation of the singer Al Jolson. Struggling with the cancer that ultimately killed him in 2004, Rev Brack was moved to another church in Hackney in the 1990s, after angrily lambasting the vicar from the pulpit.

However, back in the early 1970s the young man of God was the kind of easy going, somewhat naive, character Mackay found he could latch onto. Whether Mackay was simply looking to take advantage of his natural kindness and charitable outlook, or whether he sought genuine religious counselling will never be known.

In any case, he had recently fallen out with Father Crean and was sulking after violent rows with the Cowdreys and his mother when he phoned Rev Brack and said Marion had kicked him out. Could he come to stay? The kind-hearted vicar duly picked him up from Kings Cross and gave him a bed for the night.

However, after staying with Rev Brack for two nights, and following another row with Bert Cowdrey in Stockwell, Mackay was arrested for being drunk in the street. The following day,

15 July 1973, he was arrested again for trying to attack a homeless man with a four-foot metal stake. He was sent to Ashford Remand Centre to await a court appearance.

On 27 July, Mackay appeared at Lambeth Magistrates' Court, where he admitted to possession of a deadly weapon. Magistrates heard how the arresting officers noted his 'manic' behaviour, his racist tirades against Jews and his laughable claims that he was a 'pure Aryan'. The court was told how Mackay had once again been diagnosed as a psychopath by officials at the remand centre. By the time of his court appearance, doctors there thought he should be released to a probation hostel or another detention centre, while specialists at Broadmoor Hospital believed he should be sent back to Moss Side for further treatment. Incredibly, magistrates decided to release him back into the community, deferring sentence over the attack on the homeless man for another six months. This twelve-day spell between his arrest and the court hearing would later provide Mackay with an extraordinarily strong alibi for a murder he confessed in the most graphic terms to committing.

Despite the decision to let him go, Mackay was kept in custody until suitable living arrangements could be found. This took much longer than he'd hoped. Initially, Rev Brack refused to allow him to stay with him but caved in after repeated pleas from Mackay's solicitor. On 20 September, after nearly two months inside, he was released but when he arrived at Rev Brack's home in Finchley, he found his host had gone on holiday, perhaps intentionally. Naturally he decided to get blind drunk and went on a bender lasting more than forty-eight hours.

Four days after his release, Mackay appeared in court in Dartford, charged with being drunk and disorderly and causing damage to a public toilet. He admitted the offences and was fined £15 and ordered to pay £10.44 compensation. The next day — his 21st birthday— he was back in court in Lambeth for a further hearing over the incident with the homeless man. The court was unaware of his latest misdemeanour and the decision to defer his sentence was officially agreed.

Although the vicar had serious misgivings, Mackay moved back in with Rev Brack as a full-time lodger, paying £6 a week thanks to his latest job as a van boy with Perrings, the furniture firm. However, he was arrested again on 6 October after a particularly heavy drinking session. Mackay had fallen asleep on the train and missed his stop at East Finchley, waking up at the end of the line in High Barnet. It was the last train of the night, but he was only five miles from home so he stole a child's bicycle and began his journey back in the rain. He was stopped by police for cycling without lights — perhaps the most innocuous crime he'd ever committed — and appeared at Highgate Magistrates' Court the next day.

He was given bail for a £5 surety, but he had no money. He used his phone call to beg Rev Brack for help but the vicar refused to bail him out. As a result, Mackay spent the next three weeks in tough Pentonville Prison. It was his first real experience of living among a large adult population of hardened criminals and he was deeply unhappy about it.

He wrote to his aunt Christina saying: 'It does not ask a lot under the circumstances. I had expected last night to be bailed, but I wasn't. This made me wonder if you or Mr Brack were doing anything for me. If this is not the case then I have had it. I can do nothing to help myself in this matter.'

The probation service prepared another report, which ignored the fact that Mackay was a diagnosed psychopath. It merely said he had a 'disturbed adolescence' and was a 'volatile and unpredictable person'. The report added: 'In interview he retains a degree of calmness but there is an intenseness about him that gives the impression that he could explode if crossed on any point.' A suspended sentence was recommended. On 25 October Mackay was fined £25 and released. It was a decision that would prove to be deadly.

Despite the sentence for the offensive weapon hanging over him and his run of criminal behaviour, Rev Brack had allowed him back into his home and it was from there that Mackay would leave most mornings for his job at Perrings. But now he'd found another way to make money — robbing old ladies. The idea of carrying out 'muggings' suited him perfectly. Old women were easy targets who often carried cash in their handbags and offered little in the way of resistance. It had the added cruel advantage for Mackay that if he felt like lashing out he could do so with few repercussions.

He found his first known robbery victim during one of his frequent wanderings around London's affluent West End. He spotted Jane Comfort, an 80-year-old actress who was appearing in the world's longest-running play, *The Mousetrap*, at the Ambassadors Theatre in Covent Garden. He followed her from the street, through the stage door and into the dressing rooms before snatching her bag and making off with the princely sum of £4. He honed his technique when he targeted Jane again early in 1974 at her home in Gloucester Place, near Baker Street. Mackay approached her as she put her key in the lock and asked for directions to a non-specific museum. As it was already 9pm, she was suspicious and tried to shut the door behind her but he forced it open, knocking her to the floor. He again made off with her bag, this time containing £40.

Pleased that he had found an easier way to make a living and satisfy his lust for violence, Mackay quit his job with Perrings in January 1974. Later, he would claim it was around this time that he killed a homeless man by throwing him in the River Thames — his first 'official' victim.

He started work as a groundsman at the Tudor Sports Ground in Barnet, but continued to rob and steal. On the day he was due to reappear at Lambeth Magistrates' Court for his deferred sentence, he shaved off his eyebrows in a bizarre bid to improve his appearance. He hoped it would stand him in good stead as he was expecting to be jailed. It obviously worked as, for some reason, magistrates saw past his lengthy criminal record and handed him a two-month suspended sentence. He carried on working as a groundsman, later taking on a job at Monken Hadley Common.

On 11 February, 1974, Mackay was deprived of his liberty once again. After a drink-fuelled row at the Cowdreys' house, he was found wandering the streets, threatening to throw himself under a train. A police officer detained him in Clapham Road and sent him to Tooting Bec Hospital in South London, under the Mental Health Act.

He told doctors his partial history, excluding his time spent in Moss Side. The hospital's chief psychiatrist, Greville Gundy, swiftly diagnosed him as a psychopath and kept him under observation for two days. But because Mackay was docile and over 21 years of age, he found no grounds for forcibly detaining him. Free to leave, he immediately absconded. Later, the doctor would tell police:

> 'He admitted to me that he had felt impulsively suicidal after a drinking bout, but when he had sobered up he was glad that he had been restrained from doing so. He showed no evidence of schizophrenia or serious depression and his history and symptoms appeared to be in keeping with a personality disorder of a psychopathic type.
>
> 'I felt that there were no grounds for detaining him further at that stage and I planned to keep him for a day or so before discharging him so that he could attend an out-patient clinic in his own area. I next interviewed him on the morning of February 14, 1974. He appeared to be well settled and I felt that he could be allowed ground parole. It was my intention to discuss him with his clergyman friend and probably discharge him the following day.

However, when I visited the ward on February 15, 1974, I learned that he had absconded from the hospital the previous afternoon.'

By the time Gundy noticed his patient was missing, Mackay had already forced his way into an old woman's home and murdered her.

* * *

It was almost two weeks after Mackay left the hospital and Dr Ian Calder had spent most of the day doing routine work at Westminster Coroner's Court. He happened to be passing the mortuary at the end of his shift when a staff member raced up to him. The body of an elderly woman had been brought in by the police and they needed to establish the cause of death as a matter of urgency. Could he help? Dr Calder put all thoughts of going home out of his mind.

Dr Calder would go on to become one of Britain's leading forensic pathologists, with involvement in some of the country's most notorious cases. He examined the body of Stuart Lubbock, who died in suspicious circumstances in a swimming pool at the home of television star Michael Barrymore in 2001, and MI6 spy Gareth Williams, whose body was found mysteriously locked in a bag in his bathtub in Pimlico in 2010. But on 26 February 1974, Dr Calder was about to view the body of his first serial killer victim.

His subject's name was Isabella Fairweather Griffiths and she was 87 years old. His report was necessarily clinical and to the point. He noted how 'early putrefactive changes' were apparent on her stomach with 'advanced' changes to the back, indicating that she had been killed some time before being discovered. A knife had penetrated the chest, leaving a wound one-and-three-quarter inches long. There was bruising to the right cheek and along the jawline. More bruising was found beneath the chin and on the left side of the neck below the angle of the jaw. There was a superficial bruise running from the top of the left shoulder to the first rib and two separate bruises over the chest bone.

As well as the putrefaction, or decay, the old woman's face and shoulder had been nibbled by insects, suggesting she had lain dead for quite some time. There were small haemorrhages beneath her upper eyelids and Dr Calder noted how there were superficial haemorrhages, or 'devil's pinches', which are common in older people, on her hands but no evidence of defence wounds, suggesting the attack had been swift and left her with no chance of fighting back. The knife wound to her chest was deep and had severed the second rib. The knife then entered the lung, slicing through major blood vessels. It exited at the back of the chest in the sixth rib space, leaving a three-quarter inch wound. It didn't take long for Dr Calder to surmise that Isabella Griffiths was beaten and then killed with a knife through the chest, probably after being choked. Whoever plunged a knife into this woman had done so while she lay prone on the floor, pinning her there. With Dr Calder's help, detectives established that Isabella Griffiths was probably killed twelve days earlier on 14 February, St Valentine's Day.

Isabella Griffiths, also known as Elle, was the well-to-do widow of a surgeon. She lived alone in one of the most desirable areas of West London in a tall townhouse at 19 Cheyne Walk, just yards from the Chelsea Embankment. The road was steeped in history. Until 1760, Isabella's home had been part of the site of the mansion of Sir Hans Sloane, the Irish naturalist whose private collection was bequeathed to the nation and later formed the foundation of the British Museum.

Over the years, the mainly eighteenth-century buildings had provided sanctuary to a litany of famous names, including *Dracula* author Bram Stoker, the writer Bertrand Russell, and the actor John Barrymore. Rolling Stones frontman Mick

Jagger and his girlfriend Marianne Faithfull had moved in to Number 48 in 1968, bringing a touch of rock and roll glamour to the street. Two years earlier, Number 96 had been the venue for a top-secret meeting between British officials and members of the Provisional IRA, as well as Sinn Fein politician Gerry Adams. Details of the meeting, which was ultimately unsuccessful, were only made public several decades later. Today Chelsea Football Club owner and Russian oligarch Roman Abramovich owns a complex of homes on the street.

Isabella was a proud member of the Chelsea Gardens Guild and a recognizable figure in the community. She also had a country cottage in Haslemere, Surrey, which she would visit every year during the summer months. Fiercely independent in her widowhood, she always insisted on travelling there alone by train.

On the day she died, Isabella cashed a cheque for £25 at the Nat West Bank in the King's Road, where 17-year-old bank clerk Denise LeMay described her as looking 'shabby'. Regardless of what the teenager thought of her appearance, Isabella held a hugely successful portfolio of securities at the bank. She also had an active social life and was quite happy to walk around the streets of London on her own. She was not one for fear and self-doubt.

It was during one of her walks in February 1974 that Isabella had the misfortune of meeting Patrick Mackay. He was out of work after quitting his park keeper job at Gravesend (later Gravesham) Council and was rambling around the capital looking for victims to mug. The cruel hand of fate pointed him towards Isabella, who was walking along the road weighed down with shopping. Sizing her up as a potential mark, Mackay offered to carry her bags, which were laden with cat food. He was friendly and helpful and Isabella invited him into her home. The pair chatted for a while and he was so charming that she told him to come back in the future. Why Mackay didn't rob her there and then is anyone's guess.

For the next few weeks he called at the house regularly and Isabella would give him £5 each time to buy her groceries and cat food. It turned out to be the worst decision she ever made.

Isabella spent the early part of St Valentine's Day afternoon with friends at a party in Pimlico. She enjoyed a sherry with Eleanor Farquhar, a close friend despite the fact Eleanor was thirty-nine years her junior. They had met a decade earlier when Eleanor's mother held a party at her home in Chelsea. This latest social gathering was being hosted by Eleanor's sister Lesley Grantham.

Eleanor later said Isabella appeared 'very happy without a care in the world'. She recalled how her friend was wearing a brown hat and brown two-piece tweed suit over a brown cardigan, buttoned up to the neck. She was also wearing brown flat-heeled shoes and had a green-brown tweed overcoat, which offset her suit. Far from shabby, the tweeds were bought in Pitlochry, Scotland, which she visited every year on holiday, and which she then had made into suits and coats at her tailors in Savile Row. In addition, Isabella was carrying a brown clip bag and a nylon string shopping bag and she was wearing a string of red beads and her wedding ring.

The meal consisted of a stew and a trifle for dessert. The partygoers were treated to another glass of sherry to pour over the sponge. By the end of the party, each woman was comfortably merry. After lunch, Isabella went shopping in Victoria Street, Westminster, a twenty minute walk away. At the same time, Mackay was strolling out of Tooting Bec Hospital.

Within minutes of Isabella walking through her front door, there was a familiar knock. It was Mackay. He asked to come in but Isabella, who was probably tired from the lunch told him 'not today'. In a split-second he forced the security chain and was in the hallway. Moments later, she was dead.

The circumstances of how Isabella was found would later prove crucial to understanding Mackay's modus operandi and the tell-tale signs he left at crime scenes. He was eventually charged with one particular murder largely because of the way the scenes resembled each other.

Sadly, Isabella's body could have been discovered much sooner. Six days after the St Valentine's Day lunch, Eleanor Farquhar walked past her friend's home in Cheyne Walk. She had a habit of checking to see if milk bottles or newspapers had been left on the front porch. Isabella was a capable woman, but elderly after all. She didn't notice anything wrong and decided not to call at the house. But by 26 February Eleanor had still not seen her friend and after speaking to neighbours she became concerned.

Visiting the address with her tenant, Alan Rowlands, and a police officer, Police Constable (PC) Peter Jeffery, the trio made a gruesome discovery. PC Jeffrey later told of the considerable effort he made to gain entry to the house after finding the front door locked. Borrowing a ladder from next door, he found his way to the back garden, where he propped it up against a wall and peered into the kitchen. After spotting what looked like a body on the floor, he returned to the front of the house and kicked the door in. Once inside, he discovered the kitchen door was also locked. Borrowing a hammer from nearby builders, he smashed the door's glass panel. The officer put his hand through but there was no key on the inside. Frustrated, he used the hammer to smash the lock on the door. Unbeknown to the officer, locked doors and the removal of keys would become something of a Patrick Mackay calling card.

PC Jeffrey later described what he saw:

> 'Straight ahead of me I saw the pile of clothes on the floor. The pile was a rectangular shape. There was a piece of blue-check coloured material on the end nearest the kitchen window. I lifted up this piece of material and saw the head of a body. I pulled the material right back and saw that the body was

a female. She was lying on her back. Her head
was towards the window and her feet towards the
door. I realised that the female was dead. Her head
was slightly tilted to the right. I saw some bluey
coloured marks on her neck and underneath her
chin. There was a red substance around her mouth,
which I presumed to be blood. She was dressed in
a brown cardigan, which was buttoned up, and
a blue coat which was not buttoned, but pulled
around her. There was a bluey-coloured piece of
material covering the top half of her body and a
large piece of green material covering the lower
half of her body.'

PC Jeffrey pulled the material back over Isabella's body and
went to tell the others. Eleanor came up to identify her friend,
a horrendous task for anyone to perform, let alone while the
corpse is still in situ at the murder scene. The officer went to
alert detectives and called Dr Stuart Carne, who arrived at the
flat from a local health centre. The GP officially pronounced
Isabella dead, saying she had been for 'several days'. He noticed
that her hands were resting on her lower abdomen and thighs.

Eleanor also gave an account of the grim discovery,
remarking on the careful positioning of the body. She
recalled that Isabella's eyes were closed and noted that she
was wearing the same clothes she had been wearing to the
lunch party, suggesting she had died shortly after leaving the
group. Eleanor was not to know this, but her friend's stomach
still contained the contents of the St Valentine's Day lunch,
further confirming the date of the murder. Eleanor noticed the
shoes Isabella was wearing on the day of the party had been
removed.

'The brown shoes were immersed in water in the kitchen
sink,' she said. 'The brown handbag was on the chair beside
her and the shopping bag was hanging over the back of the

same chair. I did not see the hat or the tweed suit. As far as I can remember the handbag was open. The thing that impressed me was that her left hand was placed over her chest, it looked very beautiful indeed.'

Police realized they were dealing with a murder that had something out of the ordinary about it. During the subsequent search of the property, Detective Inspector (DI) Colin Hoye found a lower set of dentures underneath the coal fire in the hallway. Detective Constable (DC) Robert Dench noted the 'dark marks' around Isabella's throat and congealed blood on the side of her mouth. His colleague DC Michael Lee remarked that the front door had a security chain and it had still been in the locked position when it was forcefully broken. A link from the chain was lying on the floor. A padlock from a hallway cupboard had also been broken 'with some force'. The knife was not found because Mackay had taken it with him, as well as the kitchen key, which he had thrown in a nearby garden. He stole just one item from the scene — a mahogany cigarette box. Detectives were bemused by the shoes in the kitchen sink and wondered whether Isabella may even have done it herself, for some strange and unknown reason.

At first, suspicion fell on Isabella's former caretaker, a Hungarian called Hedgegus, who left her service three weeks previously. He carried out simple tasks such as sweeping leaves and bringing in the coal. He lived in a basement room rent free and was paid £1.50 a week. But Hedgegus was located and ruled out. Police had nothing to go on.

* * *

Following the death of Isabella Griffiths, Mackay continued to live with the unsuspecting Rev Brack in Finchley. If the young killer ever felt wracked by guilt, or needed to confess to the vicar or to the police, it didn't show. He carried out another home invasion on 21 February, just days before Isabella's body was discovered and only minutes away from the murder scene, in a street off the King's Road. He followed a woman to her door where he asked for a glass of water. He then asked to use the toilet, locked the woman and her elderly sister inside the bathroom and took their handbags containing £11.75.

At home, he developed a hobby, constructing and painting mini Second World War German aircraft, which he did while his head was full of violent fantasies about cooperating with the Nazi's extermination programme. Indulging his love of art, he took great care in painting swastikas on the livery and he built and painted model kits of horror icons such as Frankenstein's monster. But they were not gruesome enough for the murderous Mackay and he would burn out their eyes and stick pins in them, much to Rev Brack's concern. Yet he must have used considerable charm to remain in his property for so long, particularly because his favourite topics of conversation were his twisted thoughts on demonic possession and eternal damnation in Hell.

The vicar grew to dislike his creepy tenant and wanted him out of the house, not least because he was becoming acutely aware that his lodger urgently needed psychiatric help. The pair often quarrelled and Mackay eventually moved in with new landlords in Cedar Lawn Avenue in Barnet. The room had the advantage that it made working at Monken Hadley Common easier, and for a while he remained largely out of trouble.

On 7 July 1974, Mackay returned to the kindly vicar's home in Finchley, following a friendly phone call between the pair. Rev Brack was out, but Mackay let himself in through an open window. He made himself a simple meal but then decided to hide under the bed in his old room. Whether or not he formulated the plot before arriving at the home, or came up with it while waiting, will never be known. But after Rev Brack returned and went to sleep, Mackay crept into his room and started rifling through his pockets until the vicar woke up and chased him out of the house. In hindsight, the clergyman was lucky to escape with his life. The next time Mackay found his way into a Godly man's home he would brutally attack and kill him. Rev Brack called the police and Mackay was arrested for burglary two days later in Barnet. He appeared at Highgate Magistrates' Court on 31 July 1974.

A psychopathic killer was in police custody, but Mackay wasn't even on the radar for the murder of Isabella Griffiths. As far as detectives knew, he was a petty thief and a drunk. Just one of dozens of pitiful losers picked up on London's streets every day. If the police had looked into his past they would have discovered a disturbing history of violence coupled with a chilling diagnosis of psychopathy. And if Rev Brack had revealed all that he knew about Mackay's unpalatable habits and hobbies perhaps they might have put two and two together.

But Mackay was handed just a six-month jail term — comprising four months for the burglary and two months, previously suspended, for the earlier possession of the offensive weapon. He was sent to Wormwood Scrubs and released on 22 November 1974. The coming months would see Mackay go on a criminal rampage across London and the south east, leaving dozens of elderly people beaten and robbed and at least two more dead.

Chapter 4

I'm Sorry I Had to Hurt You

Patrick Mackay was recently out of prison with a new year on the horizon, but he had no intention of starting afresh and changing his ways. In fact, during the four months he had spent locked up, the psychopath dwelt on how easy it had been to continue his burgeoning career in petty crime even after committing a murder.

Following his arrest for the burglary at the home of Rev Ted Brack, Mackay expected to be asked about killing Isabella Griffiths at any moment. But instead of spending Christmas Day 1974 facing the rest of his life inside for murder, he passed the hours as a free man by getting blind drunk at a bail hostel in the Great North Road in Holloway, North London. Later on, he would be suspected of murdering a woman in the East End two days before Christmas 1974, but he was never charged. Yet we do know that on Boxing Day he resumed his fledgling career as a doorstep robber of old ladies.

By now, Mackay had claimed at least one life. But many more people were lucky to get away from a close encounter with him unscathed. It was never clear whether Mackay robbed simply for money or sport, or a combination of the two. His crimes often seemed to be purely cash-motivated, because he would take what he could and leave his victims virtually unharmed, although badly shaken. Yet on occasion he became gripped by a sudden and inexplicable fit of rage. Then he would wrap his hands around his victims' necks or lash out with a knife or heavy object. Later he remarked on how much he enjoyed killing, yet he never explained the degree to which he sought out that pleasure. Instead, he would often claim to have been caught up in the moment.

When Mackay finally appeared in court for his most serious offences, he was convicted of three counts of manslaughter and two robberies, and prosecutors left two other killings and twenty-three robberies to lie on file. Yet the true scale of his criminal activity is impossible to determine. It is likely that he carried out many more robberies — some possibly resulting in serious injury or even death. Mackay liked to stalk the streets of affluent Chelsea and Kensington, where he knew elderly residents were more likely to be cash-rich. The spate of attacks prompted a public outcry and forced the Metropolitan Police to set up a special unit to hunt the perpetrator. But Mackay didn't restrict his activities to those upmarket areas. He would roam all over London, as well as parts of Kent. Because his life was ruled by impulse, it's inevitable that he would also have committed similar offences in those places.

Mugging was a crime that seemed to suit his needs perfectly, both from a financial point of view and in terms of satisfying his violent urges. It was much more enjoyable than the sneaky commercial burglaries he sometimes carried out in Gravesend, and it reminded him of the buzz he got when bullying girls in the school playground. Back then, he would barge into a schoolgirl's shoulder and send her crashing to the ground, just for a laugh. Now, he would force his way through an old woman's front door and demand money with menaces. If he felt his victims were messing him around, he would threaten them or grab them by the arms and march them through their own homes until they handed over cash or valuables.

After the bungled burglary at Rev Brack's home, Mackay decided to focus on this style of crime. One of his first targets just so happened to be one of his wealthiest — Lady Becher. Mackay didn't know who she was of course, he simply spotted her out and about and followed her home to Wilton Street, Belgravia. It was a classic Mackay doorstep robbery. Lady Becher was about to put her key in the lock when he approached, grabbed her by the throat and pulled out a knife. He got away with £115 and a silver medallion worth £85. He committed an almost identical doorstep robbery four days later in Tite Street, Chelsea.

Sometimes, in lieu of brute force, he would offer to carry his victim's bags or pretend to have lost his keys to apartments in the communal building. The friendly approach had served him well with Isabella Griffiths, allowing him to gain her confidence. Another favourite ruse was to knock at a door feigning illness and ask for a glass of water.

Detectives began plotting the crimes on a map, marking each location with a red dot. Many of the robberies were around the King's Road area so they suspected that whoever was targeting old ladies had also murdered Isabella Griffiths. They also feared — correctly — that the doorstop robber would kill again.

On 15 February 1975, one day after the first anniversary of the attack on Isabella Griffiths, Mackay forced his way into the home of another elderly widow, 79-year-old Margaret Diver. Her flat was also off the King's Road, in Old Church Street. She was through the front gate and about half way up the steps to the front door when she heard the gate open behind her and an unfamiliar voice bark, 'I want to speak to you about your husband.'

She turned round and the dead-eyed Mackay was staring back at her. 'I have no husband,' she replied nervously. 'What name do you want?'

Pausing for a moment, Mackay said 'Jackson.'

'There's no-one of that name living here,' Margaret shot back.

'Are you sure?' he asked.

Margaret said she was sure and Mackay seemed to turn away and go back down the stairs. But as she entered the front door he followed her in quickly and slammed it behind him. With both hands over her face, he forced her to the floor. 'If you make a noise it will be worse for you,' he hissed.

He dragged his terrified victim by her coat collar through the hallway and into the kitchen. Once there he helped Margaret to her feet and seemed for a moment to forget what he was doing. He ordered her to make him a cup of tea and insisted she drink one too. The pair made awkward small talk, and two or three times during the conversation Mackay mentioned he was an outpatient at Tooting Bec Hospital. Finally, after what seemed like an age, he put down his cup.

'I'll wait thirty seconds and I'll go. You mustn't move on any account,' he said. Then as suddenly as he had arrived, he left. Margaret sat frozen to the spot until she was sure he'd left the building, then shaking like a leaf she rushed to a neighbouring flat and pounded on the door for help.

Margaret Diver had just taken afternoon tea with a psychopathic killer. Although she didn't know, she had been perilously close to suffering the same fate as Isabella Griffiths. Having been bundled to the floor and dragged along like a rag doll, Margaret was left with a bruised nose and lip and facial swelling. Fortunately, her ordeal ended without her coming to serious physical harm, although there is little doubt the incident left her with deep psychological scars for the remaining years of her life. Mackay got away with a bag, a purse, a watch, a bus pass, some meat coupons and £1.25 in cash. Margaret was able to give a description of her attacker, although it wasn't particularly accurate — about 5ft 6ins, late 20s, with brown curly hair which fell on his forehead, a 'small round face' with pink cheeks, brown eyes, 'florid complexion' and 'not very smartly dressed'.

She added that Mackay made a habit of saying 'dear' at the end of every sentence. 'Just before he left he said, "I'm sorry I had to hurt you dear." I was really frightened. I thought he was going to kill me.'

The robbery of Margaret Diver was later to form a key part of the evidence against Mackay because during the course of the crime he carelessly left his thumbprint on a teaspoon. However, neither that clue, nor the reckless admission that he had spent time in Tooting Bec Hospital, led to his immediate arrest.

It is unclear exactly when detectives first made enquiries at the hospital. Dr Greville Gundy's statement detailing how Mackay absconded on the day Isabella Griffiths was killed was only taken after his final arrest and several months after the Margaret Diver robbery. This would suggest the robber's mental health did not form a significant line of enquiry from an early stage. If it had done so, detectives may well have spotted that a diagnosed psychopath named Patrick Mackay absconded on the very day Isabella Griffiths was killed, giving them an obvious suspect for that and the robberies. Unfortunately, the thumbprint would turn up as a match for Mackay only after he had killed two more people.

On 6 March 1975, Mackay again chanced the wrath of God by carrying out a crime in a church. In what was a relatively minor offence for him, he walked in to Christ Church in Chelsea and rifled through the pockets of the verger's jacket, which was hanging on a banister. But the following day he returned to more serious crime, carrying out another brutal robbery.

Ilma Lewis, a 68-year-old Uruguayan journalist, had been shopping in Victoria after work and was about to let herself in to her flat in Chesham Street, Belgravia. Like most of the streets Mackay stalked, it had more than a few well-heeled residents, including several MPs and the Spanish Embassy, and it would later become home to former Prime Minister Margaret Thatcher.

Mackay attacked just before 4pm, following Ilma into the house, just as she walked through the front door. As she got to the top of the stairs she sensed someone was behind her, but before she could do anything he grabbed her and put both of his hands across her face, with one over her mouth so she couldn't speak.

'How much money have you got in your bag?' he demanded.

Ilma was forced to mumble through his hand that she only had £10.

'You're not lying to me? Don't lie to me or else I'll kill you,' replied Mackay. 'Drop your bag.'

She hesitated, which made him angry. He squeezed her face as hard as he could and repeated his demand.

'You live downstairs don't you?' he asked. Ilma shook her head.

'I don't like doing this,' said Mackay. 'I'll kill you but I don't want to.'

He then said he was leaving and warned her not to look at him or he would kill her. He shoved her in the face when she instinctively turned to watch him walk away. 'Give me a start and call the police,' he ordered before squeezing her face again, perhaps debating whether or not to take it further. Then he picked up her handbag and ran out into Lyle Street.

Mackay got away with £25 in cash, two return tickets to Penrith from Victoria Coach Station, one Uruguayan Press Association card, a Lloyds Bank cheque card, a brown wallet, two cheque books, a Boots cash voucher for £1.50, a pair of glasses and various membership cards, as well as a wristwatch. It was not much of a haul, but enough to pay for his booze for the day. His victim was left utterly petrified.

Police now knew the robber of old ladies had a habit of telling his victims how much he regretted his violent acts. 'I don't like doing this,' he would repeat. But if Mackay really did feel bad about hurting people he would have stopped after the murder of Isabella Griffiths and focused on his job as a groundsman or, better still, handed himself in. Instead, four days after robbing Ilma Lewis, on 10 March 1975, he devoured an entire bottle of scotch and went looking for another victim outside the luxury department store Harrods, in Knightsbridge.

Failing to find a suitable candidate, he made his way to nearby Lowndes Square, where he saw 89-year-old Adele Price preparing to enter the front door of her grand Victorian terraced home, where she lived in a first-floor flat. Mackay approached from behind, jangling his keys. Adele Price, very politely, held the door open for him.

Lowndes Square is a stone's throw from Harrods, its rival luxury department store Harvey Nichols and Knightsbridge tube station, so naturally its grand white stucco terraces only attract the finest residents, including politicians and members of the aristocracy. Until Mackay showed up, the most unsavoury person to spend time in one of the buildings was probably the British fascist Sir Oswald Mosley, who lived in Lowndes Square for most of his life, until he died in 1980. It is still a magnet for the mega-wealthy and, as in Cheyne Walk, the Russian oligarch Roman Abramovich has owned a complex of flats on the square.

Adele Price shared the flat with her 25-year-old granddaughter Jane Matheson, a secretary. When Jane returned home at about 5.50pm she entered the communal hallway but found the Chubb lock to her grandma's home was already open. She thought her grandmother had simply forgotten to lock it but after trying to turn the Yale lock, Jane found the latch was up and the door wouldn't open. 'Grandma never ever leaves the latch up in case there is a fire and the firemen can't get in,' she explained later.

Jane knocked and waited for the elderly woman to make her way to the door. But after a while she noticed that either the television or radio must be on inside the flat, because she could hear male voices. She also heard a door open or close. Confused, she walked out of sight of the flat and went back to the front of the house to use the buzzer.

In a bold move, Mackay stepped out of the flat and walked down to the lobby. He was almost as confused as Jane. Later, he would confess to falling asleep in the afterglow of his crime and waking up bewildered when he heard the door. When he saw Jane on the doorstep, he decided to put on a northern accent in an effort to disguise himself. 'He came towards the front door and I asked him if he had seen anyone open the door on the first floor because I live there with my grandmother and couldn't get in,' Jane would tell police later. 'He said, "I did see a man open and close the door" and that I should call the porter. I asked this man if he would come upstairs with me in case there was someone in the flat because I was worried. He seemed in a hurry and told me to ring the porter. He then walked off in the direction of Knightsbridge. I don't know whether he had a car.' Jane described him as 'middle height, sandy blond hair, slightly thinning at front, round face. I think he had a north country accent, wearing a dark coloured raincoat. I think he was about 25 years to 30 years. I think he had his hands in his pockets.' Later on she would provide a more specific description of Mackay. She said he was clean shaven with a 'fresh sort of complexion', about 5ft 10ins, with a parting in his hair on the left side and no moustache or glasses.

Jane called on her neighbours, Ann and Nick Parry. The trio went upstairs and tried the Yale lock again. This time it opened. The lights were on in the hall, the curtains were drawn and the kitchen door was open. There was a screwdriver on the table, apparently left behind by Mackay. 'On the side table with the flaps down, I noticed a radio case and her bundle of keys,' Jane told officers. 'I thought it odd because Grandma is impeccably tidy. I saw the top drawer of a little set of drawers near my camp bed was open. I went back to the living room door and Grandma's bedroom door was closed and Anne found it was locked and opened it. She gasped and her eyes widened and I knew something had happened to Grandma, and I flung myself down onto the living room sofa. Nick took me upstairs.'

The police and ambulance service were called. Initially medics believed there was nothing suspicious about the scene, and if it had not been for the quick-thinking PC Alan MacGregor from Gerald Road Police Station, vital evidence could have been lost. One of the ambulance men told him, 'She's gone mate, but she is still a little bit warm, so we will take her.' But MacGregor was not convinced, as he explained later:

> 'They started to lift her shoulders and the air expired from her body and a greenish white fluid came from her mouth in a trickle. I had noticed that the body was fully dressed in street clothing and that her handbag was lying on the floor of the bedroom to the right of the body as I viewed it. There was also a screwed-up letter lying on a seat in front of a table which stood against the right-hand wall. From information that I had previously been given regarding police action in similar circumstances, I advised the ambulance men not to remove the body or disturb it any further.
>
> 'They lowered the head and shoulders of the body to the floor and stepped back. I then spoke to Miss Parry and established that she had found the body in the presence of the granddaughter of the dead woman, who had asked her to look in the flat with her, as she could not find her grandmother when she had first looked by herself. I was asked by the ambulance men if they could remove the body. I told them to leave the body as it was.'

MacGregor's decision would later prove instrumental in proving Mackay committed the crime. Forensic teams quickly moved in to gather evidence and officers lifted one of Mackay's prints from the screwed-up letter. Another officer noticed the key in the outside lock of the bedroom door, confirming suspicions that Adele Price's death was unnatural. He also spotted a white metal earring set with green stones out of place in a fruit bowl on a table to the right of the lounge doors. In the lounge, the curtains were drawn, the door leading to the kitchen was open and the kitchen door, which led to a balcony area, was also open. The doors of a drinks cabinet were wide open and a nylon stocking was hanging from a tin. Later, when he was questioned about the stocking, Mackay would make a strange comment that appeared to link him to other crimes. On a small table there were two radio ear plugs, as used with a transistor radio, and a radio case but no radio. Near the case was a beige-coloured purse. The Chubb and Yale keys, both on a piece of string, were found on a glass-topped table alongside Mackay's screwdriver. The killer must have been intending to take them with him.

Jane officially identified her grandmother's body at the coroner's court. She later added to her statement: 'I have been asked whether a radio would have been in my grandmother's bedroom. I can only say that I don't know. She had a little radio so that she could carry it about with her from room to room. I don't know where it would have been left. My radio, the Panasonic one, was always in the living room. I have also been asked whether or not the curtains in the living room can be closed by using the puller cord. This cord has always worked and the curtains were always closed by using it.' Once again, these details would become important when detectives later sought to confirm Mackay's confession and to verify his strange behaviour after the crime.

Pathologist Keith Simpson concluded that Adele Price died from asphyxia due to manual strangulation. She was still wearing her outdoor coat, suggesting there had been just moments between her walking in and being killed. The investigation was turned over to Detective Superintendent (DSUP) John Bland, deputy head of CID for London's

A Division. Bland was already overseeing the efforts to stop the West End mugger. Now his worst fears had come true — the killer of Isabella Griffiths had struck again. Bland later gave MacGregor a commendation for his quick thinking in preserving the murder scene.

Over the course of three months in early 1975 Mackay had stolen cash, jewellery and other items from his victims valued at about £2,000. However, he failed to benefit in full because he dumped valuable gems from at least one robbery, believing they were fake. With a certain degree of boldness, he kept some of his loot under a loose floorboard in the Cowdreys' front room in Stockwell. On one occasion, Bert Cowdrey found two watches and jewellery in the space. He confronted Mackay, who said he was looking after them for a friend. For whatever reason, Bert did not think to tell the police about his suspicions. It was another lost opportunity. If he had done so, Mackay's crime spree might have been brought to an end.

* * *

Two days after the murder of Adele Price, British Transport Police officer PC John Creighton was called to Stockwell tube station where a man had been seen walking into a northbound Northern Line tunnel towards Oval. Staff turned off the electricity in the rails and forcibly detained him in a maintenance hut. Creighton recognized the trespasser, who he knew as Peter McCann, an alias frequently used by Mackay. The officer asked him what he was doing. 'I'm trying to kill myself,' replied Mackay. Days after claiming another life, he was once again feeling sorry for himself. Once again, efforts to end his own life had fallen short. Whether or not he ever really intended to die is open to question. Perhaps it was just a cry for help and a way to seek treatment for his mental health problems without having to admit what he had done. If so, the latest incident was partially successful, because he was indeed taken to a psychiatric hospital. Before that, PC Creighton asked Mackay why he was putting his life in danger:

> 'He told me he was trying to commit suicide, by walking down the tunnel, hoping that a train would come and run him over. I questioned him further and he told me that he was fed up with life and that everybody was against him. We detained McCann at about 12.10am and transported him by police van to Kensington Police Station, arriving at 12.25am. Whilst in the van we talked about what would have happened if the train had come along and McCann said that he realized what effect it could have had on the driver and he would not want to do that. He talked of his mother saying that she would be upset if he had committed suicide and that she knew he had tried before.'

Double killer Mackay was once again in the hands of the law. And once again, he had been detained just days after committing a murder. Further enquiries by the officer uncovered Mackay's real name, but he claimed he had officially changed it to McCann about a month earlier. Mackay told the officer he was working in the Chicken Inn in Leicester Square as a kitchen porter, which was true, but said he was living at Cedar Lawn Avenue, Barnet, which was no longer true. He was living in the bail hostel in Holloway.

'He talked about his sister, did not say a name, and said that she avoided him and that once when he had spoken to her she looked at him as if he were a devil,' said Creighton. 'He talked about a priest who was trying to help him. He said that the priest understood him.' If Mackay was once again mentioning a holy man in a bid to elicit sympathy, it may have worked. 'I can't remember any mention of where the priest lived or his name,' added Creighton. 'We made a lot of general conversation about how long he was going to be there and all during this he chain smoked. He mentioned having first tried suicide at the age of 11 by taking an overdose of tablets and trying to throw himself off a block of flats, but someone grabbed him at the last moment.'

Mackay was taken to the psychiatric wing of the South Western Hospital in Stockwell, where he was left in the care of a Dr Barclay. Even though police now knew his real name, Mackay was booked in at the hospital under the name McCann. The following day, he tried to strangle himself with a pyjama cord, which caused him to pass out. When he came to, a three-day observation order was made by Dr Michael Pritchard. Yet, despite keeping him in, the hospital didn't uncover his full medical or criminal history and didn't find out about his stint in Moss Side. Dr Pritchard diagnosed Mackay as a psychopath but, as usual, there were no grounds for his further detention and he was released on 18 March 1975. Despite suggestions the West End robber had previously been treated at Tooting Bec Hospital, the police were clearly not keeping an eye on newcomers to London's mental health units.

Over the next two days, Mackay carried out three more robberies, finally crashing at the Cowdreys' home in Stockwell drunk and exhausted. One day after that, he killed again. This time Mackay's victim would not die during a random attack. Instead, he sought out one of the few men who had shown him kindness during his troubled youth — Father Anthony Crean — and brutally ended his life.

Chapter 5

Bloodbath

'There's nothing more to be said,' shouted Father Crean as he climbed back into his car. As he drove away, he watched Mackay staring blankly in the rear-view mirror and shuddered under his creepy glare. At this point Father Crean had no reason to fear Mackay but nor did he have any desire to see the young man again. As a condition of not being sent to prison, Mackay had agreed to pay back the £80 he swindled using the cheque he stole in June 1973. But several months later, Father Crean was still waiting for a single penny. Now he had shown up unannounced and full of excuses Father Crean felt it was time to cut his losses. He no longer trusted the troubled young drifter.

Shorne in Kent was, and still is, the quintessential English village with a tight-knit community. It has three pubs — the Rose and Crown, the See Ho and the Copperfield — as well as a post office, GP surgery and convenience store, all of which Father Crean visited on a near daily basis for a chat and to keep up to date with village news.

His seventeenth-century cottage, Malthouse, sat just behind St Peter and St Paul's Church, which neighboured St Katherine's convent, of which he was chaplain. St Katherine's housed twelve nuns, who in turn oversaw St Joseph's children's home.

Although Father Crean lived alone at Malthouse, the sisters, governed by prioress Sister Therese Simon, prepared his meals and left them each day on a tray in the convent's kitchen for him to collect. Father Crean would return the dirty dishes.

It was an existence characterized by a dull but nonetheless satisfying routine. Father Crean had already lived an interesting life, beginning his career in the clergy in Spain during the Civil War in the 1930s, then living in Gibraltar and later making frequent trips to the United States. He had only returned to England in 1967 and now he preferred life at a slower pace, which allowed him to indulge his passions for repairing clocks and gardening. Small and wiry — he was only five feet tall — Father Crean was intelligent but feisty. A few villagers found him too feisty, nicknaming him 'Holy Joe' and finding him aggressive and hard to get along with. His way of dealing with people he had annoyed was simply to ignore them or become increasingly impolite. Still, he got on well with most of the locals and could be seen most mornings tending to the cottage's meticulously well-kept lawns and flower beds.

Father Crean first met Mackay while walking in the woods around Shorne in May 1973, shortly after the latter's release from Moss Side. The spot was three miles from Mackay's mother's home in Gravesend and a stone's throw from Malthouse. The pair struck up a conversation and although Mackay kept the details of his turbulent and violent past to himself there was no mistaking the forlorn air and obvious aimlessness of the lanky youth. Father Crean prided himself on his empathy and kindness towards the needy and after a couple of minutes of idle chatter he identified Mackay as the kind of waif he might be able help. They immediately headed to the pub. Perhaps a copious amount of beer and whisky in the Rose and Crown was not the kind of help Patrick Mackay needed, but following that boozy afternoon the pair embarked on a short-lived friendship.

The stolen cheque incident was hardly a complex case for Gravesend CID. Detective Sergeant (DS) Bob Brown knew of

Mackay because of the many violent bust ups at his family home. He also knew about his friendship with Father Crean. When a priest starts hanging around with a local criminal, people tend to talk. Coupled with the bank clerk's description of the crook who handed in the cheque, the case was closed almost as soon as it was opened.

When Father Crean was told of Mackay's arrest he asked for the charges to be dropped, although he surely must have realized when he made the complaint that his young friend would be the prime suspect. Perhaps he believed a few hours in the cells would give him a short, sharp shock, but he misjudged the attitude of the police. DI Ken Tappenden of Gravesend CID took one look at Mackay's criminal and mental health record and decided to press charges.

Mackay was in deep fear of being sent back to Moss Side, but he admitted his guilt and was handed a conditional discharge at Northfleet Magistrates' Court in June 1973. He was fined £20 for breaking and entering and told to repay the £80 at £7 a week. He resumed his friendship with Father Crean almost immediately after the hearing, but it fizzled out when Mackay failed to repay any money. The pair were seen talking in the street about eight months later, before Father Crean stormed off in his car. It was the last time they would be seen together.

Nearly a year later, on 21 March 1975, Father Crean failed to collect his dinner from the convent. The reason, it later transpired, was that he had been hacked to death with an axe.

* * *

Why did Patrick Mackay have such close relationships with two priests, Reverend Ted Brack and Father Anthony Crean? It must have been more than coincidence. It is possible Mackay genuinely wanted to live up to his father's desire to raise a God-fearing son. Realistically it was probably because he saw religious figures as a soft target, identifying their generosity and propensity for forgiveness as a weakness.

The statement made to police by Tooting Bec Hospital's head psychiatrist Greville Gundy might provide a clue. He told detectives he was in touch with Mackay's 'clergyman friend', namely Rev Brack. Gundy had felt more confident about discharging his patient because he appeared to have responsible friends in the community. Mackay would mention his association with men of the cloth to the police, possibly to make himself a more sympathetic figure to the authorities. He certainly spoke of Rev Brack when he was arrested during the incident in the London Underground after killing Adele Price. It could be that he found these ecclesiastical buddies, not by chance, but by seeking them out intentionally. After all, it was he who had initiated the move to Rev Brack's home in Finchley. Did he also engineer the encounter with Father Crean as the priest took his routine daily walk around the village?

One other possible explanation is that Mackay was homosexual and he found more than simple companionship with the two men. Certainly Mackay seemed to have few, if any, female friends and there is no evidence that he ever had a girlfriend. He apparently bragged about attending orgies and claimed to have had several female sexual partners. But if this was true, they never came out of the woodwork to tell their stories after he was arrested and none featured in his prison memoir. The only people with whom Mackay ever appeared to have a close bond were the priests, his own family members and the Cowdrey family. That being said, there has never been any suggestion that either Rev Brack or Father Crean was gay.

For their part, the Cowdrey boys had their own opinions about Mackay's relationships with the two men, although they phrased their views in considerably more vulgar terms. The younger lads joked about Mackay's bond with Father Crean and crudely labelled the priest a 'shit-stabber'. Mackay furiously denied the relationship was sexual. But whatever the truth of the matter, Mackay and Father Crean met regularly for a few weeks in 1973, mostly in the pub, and Mackay introduced the priest to his family and his mother's new fiancé.

One certainty is that the relationship with Father Crean revolved around alcohol. Both men were heavy drinkers, and in January 1972 the priest had been fined £25 and banned from the road for twelve months for drink driving. Mackay's 17-year-old sister, Heather, later told police: 'A vicar, or a man wearing a dog collar, came to our house at Frobisher Way, Gravesend. I cannot remember too much about the incident but I went through the lounge and Patrick was with the man. They were sitting in chairs and there were empty cans which had contained beer on the floor. I think Patrick introduced me to the vicar but I cannot remember his name now.'

By the time Mackay decided to revisit Father Crean for the final occasion in March 1975 the 22-year-old had already killed at least two women and more than half a dozen opportunities to stop his crime spree had been missed. Nobody was on his trail and there was not a hint of suspicion that he was anything more than a vagrant or a mentally unwell drifter and alcoholic who indulged in occasional petty crime.

Ten days after the murder of Adele Price, during which he had spent another short spell in a psychiatric hospital, Mackay turned up at the Cowdreys' family home in Grantham Road, Stockwell, to fulfil a promise to take the children to a nearby fair.

Leigh Cowdrey, who was 16 at the time, later told police he had known Mackay for about six years, after he found him sleeping rough in a derelict house in Wandsworth. Leigh, who lived with his mum, dad, two brothers and two of his three sisters, said it was not unusual for Mackay to turn up at their house out of the blue. As the children, Terry, 18, Martin 14, Beverley, 12, Tina, 9 and a neighbour's child Sally, waited for him in the front room, Martin, who had learning difficulties, mentioned that he had been in the derelict house nearby, which used to be lived in by the Vicar of St Andrew's Church. On hearing the word 'vicar', Mackay erupted. 'He leapt up from his chair and said to Martin, "Don't you ever mention that word again to me,"' recalled Leigh. 'He said he was going down to see a vicar. He didn't say where to, who it was or what he was going to do.' After that everyone except Terry went to the fair.

Mackay had around £15 cash with him and the group stayed at the fair for about an hour. Then Mackay and Leigh went to The Clarence pub in Stockwell to meet Bert, Vi and Terry while the youngsters went home. Leigh said Mackay wore a suede coat with imitation fur collar, dark red trousers and brown suede shoes. After a couple of beers, Mackay again mentioned his plans for the following day. 'Patrick mentioned that he was going to Kent to do some tree felling,' said Leigh. 'Patrick bought a few rounds of drinks during the course of the evening and he left to go home with us about 11pm. I would say that Patrick was well on the way to being drunk.' At home, they chatted before heading to bed. Mackay slept on the couch and by the time Leigh got up the following morning at 10.30am, he'd gone.

Vi Cowdrey, who later confessed that she knew nothing about his spells in psychiatric hospitals, had noticed a number of cuts and bruises on his right hand, which appeared to be turning septic. They were possibly from the Adele Price killing. At the Clarence, he had told Vi that he had 'business to attend to' in Kent the next day. What legitimate business she thought the drunken, violent, thieving Mackay had planned in Kent is not clear.

Bert Cowdrey also gave an account to police. He said Mackay spent most of the evening buying rounds of drinks. 'He always seemed to have plenty of money with him,' he said. Mackay had also told Bert of his plans to go 'tree felling' the next day. The following afternoon, Mackay boarded a train from Waterloo to Gravesend. He was armed with two kitchen knives. Not enough to fell a tree, but sufficient to kill a vicar.

Mackay arrived in Gravesend just under an hour after leaving Waterloo. He crept into his mother's house through the back door, startling her. He was clutching a plucked chicken, which she eventually agreed to cook after he told her he would otherwise roast it himself on an open fire on nearby waste ground. He then said he was going for a walk and would be back later that evening.

For Father Crean the morning had been like any other. He said Mass as usual at 7.30am and Sister Therese spoke to him just before 8am about convent business. She saw him again at about 4.30pm, assiduously mowing the lawn and placing the cuttings on a small bonfire. He then went for a stroll with his faithful Jack Russell, Jacko, in tow.

Schoolboy Michael Bowles, and his friends, saw Father Crean walking the dog near the Rose and Crown at about 4.45pm. They cycled past and said hello. Father Crean returned the greeting. Godfrey Martin, 35, had recently bought the old primary school and converted it into a house. He stopped to speak to Father Crean as he passed outside at about 5.20pm. 'I always found him to be a friendly intelligent man and have spent many hours in conversation with him,' he recalled later. 'Father Crean approached me and waved. It was obvious that he wanted a chat, so I waited for him. We then both stood talking together at the entrance to the rough ground which serves as a car park opposite the old school premises. The conversation lasted for five or ten minutes.' The next person to see Father Crean alive would be Patrick Mackay.

At 6.10pm, Sister Therese noticed Father Crean had not collected his supper tray. Just before 7pm, she noticed that Jacko was on the lawn alone. By 8.15pm the supper tray had still not been collected. Concerned, she looked out across the lawn and noticed the downstairs lights were on and the curtains were drawn. The upstairs lights appeared to be off. She took the tray over to the cottage but found both doors locked. She was surprised because Father Crean usually kept the cottage unlocked, but she left the tray outside the door and went back to the convent to fetch the keys.

When Sister Therese finally got into the cottage, she saw no sign of Father Crean. Thinking it unusual, she collected the used lunch dishes from the kitchen and poked her head into his ground-floor bedroom. The light was on and his waistcoat was lying on the bed. After making sure that Jacko was locked inside, Sister Therese went back to the convent, leaving the door unlocked. Once at the convent, she made a call to local police to see if the Father had been in any trouble. He hadn't.

On the same day, Mick Derrington, a 21-year-old child care officer from Leicester, was visiting St Joseph's and lodging at Malthouse with Father Crean. He had gone to the convent for a cup of tea and to watch television at about 5pm. At 6.45pm, the doorbell rang. It was a local woman, Isabel Cane, who had found Jacko running around outside. Mick later recalled him being 'snappy'. The dog dutifully followed him to the cottage.

Mick was keen to get back to the convent to carry on watching his programme and as he was nervous around the agitated dog, he shut Jacko in the grounds and didn't enter the cottage. He noticed that the lights were on and the curtains were drawn, so he assumed Father Crean would let Jacko inside in due course. Mick then went back to the convent and didn't return to the cottage until after Sister Therese's visit.

When he did finally decide to turn in, he called out to Father Crean before going upstairs, but there was no reply. He noticed Jacko was now sitting in an armchair. 'He growled at me so I shut the study door and went up to my room,' he said. 'I had been reading a book and at about midnight I thought that I had better do something because I had not heard Father Crean in the cottage. I got partially dressed and went downstairs. I searched through every room in the cottage downstairs, except the room I now know is the downstairs bathroom. At the time I thought it was a cupboard because there is an upstairs bathroom.'

Mick went back to the convent and roused the sisters. They feared Father Crean may have had an accident on the road, even though his car was parked outside the cottage. Sister Therese and Mick returned to the cottage. She quickly became uneasy. Father Crean normally went to bed between 10.30pm and 11pm but the lights were on and the curtains were drawn. She saw his waistcoat had been abandoned on the bed, although the priest was normally very tidy. She then noticed the bathroom, which Mick had mistaken for a cupboard. It was closed although Father Crean normally left the door wide open. Sister Therese opened the door, screamed and ran out the house.

'I looked into the bathroom and in the bath I saw what I thought was clothing,' said Mick. 'I ran after Sister Therese and tried to calm her down. I then returned alone to the cottage and went into the bathroom and I saw blood and saw Father Crean laying in the bath. He appeared to be completely submerged in the water.'

The room was a bloodbath. Father Crean was lying face up, fully clothed in the tub, his face partially covered by water and almost unrecognizable thanks to a number of horrific wounds. A towel had been placed over his head, but underneath the material his brain was exposed. Forensic pathologists would later find brain tissue on his fingers, suggesting he had at some point reached into the open wound. The bath had been filled with water, which was now crimson. Father Crean had a rosary draped over his right hand.

DI Ken Tappenden was at a black-tie event more than fourteen miles away in Maidstone when the alert first came in to say Father Crean was missing. He would later describe the horrendous scene officers encountered at the cottage. 'We had a call about 8.30pm to say Father Crean had not returned home, although his Jack Russell had,' he would explain when interviewed for the documentary, *Born to Kill: The Devil's Disciple*. 'That was the only thing that put anything of suspicion in one's mind. Nothing came in for another couple of hours and eventually we get another call saying he still isn't home and now it's dark and people are beginning to get quite worried about it. A number of us go straight to the scene, straight from the hotel in our DJs.'

By the time they arrived, Father Crean's horribly mutilated body had already been discovered. 'A nun was actually screaming,' said DI Tappenden. 'And it would appear that the priest had been found dead, in a bath filled with blood. He was in the bath in his duffle coat, he was in his Wellingtons, and he had a woolly hat on.' Officers quickly located the murder weapon — a small wooden-handled axe covered in blood. They believed the blunt end had been used to crack his skull. 'I know you get used to it,' said Tappenden, 'but every now and again you find a murder scene that is disturbing. When you see the ferocity in which he was attacked and killed you can't help but keep thinking about it.'

Home Office pathologist James Cameron was called out from the London Hospital Medical College at 4.20am to examine the scene. He noted there was 'much blood-staining' on the bath and 'all over the wall'. A post-mortem examination was carried out at 6am at Gravesend and North Kent Hospital.

Father Crean had been found wearing his left Wellington boot, grey socks, blue oversocks, belted trousers and underpants. A scarf was round his neck, suggesting he had been attacked moments after getting home. Dr Cameron's report suggested that Father Crean had been given little opportunity to stop the ferocious assault and would have spent some time in pain before he died.

'In the right hand there appeared to be blood-stained brain tissue and there was dried blood in the left hand, but no rings were present on either hand and there were no defence marks on either hand,' wrote the pathologist. The attack had been unusually savage, even by Mackay's standards. Dr Cameron found at least nineteen wounds on Father Crean's body. They included bruising of the middle of the chest, bruising to the upper chest, bruising behind the lower left arm, a half-inch stab wound to the centre of the lower neck, a half-inch stab wound three inches below the left ear, and a superficial stab wound, undercut from left to right, below the left jaw. There was a one-and-a-half inch cut over the left eyebrow, a cut over the outer corner of the left eye, a fracture of the nose, and bruises on the neck.

One of the most serious wounds was a ragged chasm in the centre of the forehead, exposing Father Crean's brain and skull. There was also a semi-circular wound to the upper left forehead, a T-shaped wound slightly to the left of the hairline, a Y-shaped wound to the upper right forehead and two semi-circular wounds to the right of the top of the head. There were wounds, three and five inches respectively, above the right ear and a fracture of the left cheekbone.

Internally, Dr Cameron found more injuries, including a cut lip, loose and fractured teeth, bruising of the tongue, bruising to the right collar bone, skull fractures and bruising and cuts to the brain. Father Crean's lungs were waterlogged and showed evidence of a wound in the right upper chest, with bleeding into the chest cavity. The pathologist concluded that the axe found at the scene was 'used with considerable force against the head'. He added: 'There were multiple superficial stab wounds, only one of which penetrated any depth, the stab wounds in themselves having no bearing on the cause of death.' That cause was given as 'cerebral contusions and lacerations and a compound fractured skull'. Before the post-mortem was even complete, police were already hunting for Patrick Mackay.

DI Ken Tappenden immediately remembered Father Crean from the cheque theft case two years earlier. The perpetrator then was Mackay and he thought it would be too much of a coincidence to suspect that anyone else would have targeted the kindly village priest in such a savage and apparently motiveless attack. DC Mick Whitlock and DS Bob Brown were called to Tappenden's office at about 3am and told to find him. Brown had arrested him once before and was determined to do so again.

Following the killing, Mackay behaved in a typically haphazard fashion. He went back to his mother's house to eat the chicken, but he tucked in half-heartedly and then decided he wasn't hungry. His mother wrapped the leftovers in tin foil and he left. He then went to the local cinema to watch *Death Wish*, the controversial new film starring Charles Bronson. The plot was about a man who becomes a blood-thirsty vigilante after his wife is murdered. It was tame fare for a serial killer who had just seen off his third and final official victim. Mackay spent almost all of his remaining money on the ticket and a box of popcorn.

He turned up at Gravesend train station at about 8.10pm, telling the ticket officers he had just 15 ½ pence in his pocket. Ticket officer Malcolm Titshall said Mackay seemed to be 'hurrying' and was 'in a bit of a flap'.

Mackay asked Titshall what he could do about getting a ticket. 'I asked him if there was anyone we could contact and he said "No". Then he said he was living with someone but he couldn't contact them by telephone. I said the only thing you can do is travel up to London and give them your name and address when you get there. He said, "Okay, I'll do that and come in tomorrow and pay the money."' After speaking to the ticket collector, he went to the platform and a few minutes later boarded a train.

Sightings of Mackay making his way around Shorne and Gravesend that evening confirmed Father Crean had already been dead in the bath when Sister Therese and then Mick Derrington came into the cottage after 8pm. Mackay would later describe how Jacko ran out of the cottage shortly before the attack, meaning the priest must have been killed sometime after 5.20pm, when he was last seen in the village, and before 6.45pm when Mick brought the dog back to the cottage grounds. If Mick had decided not to watch television at the convent Mackay would probably have been scared off before Father Crean came home, although there is also the possibility that the youth worker himself would have been killed.

Officers Brown and Whitlock turned up at Marion Mackay's house in Frobisher Way shortly before dawn. She lied, telling the detectives she hadn't seen her son for months. Even when Mackay later admitted going to the house, Marion would not go back on her lies. 'If Patrick says he went to the house then he went, but I did not see him. He must have imagined he saw me,' she said. 'Maybe he wanted to see me so much that he thought he saw me.' Even then, with Mackay facing a murder charge, she could see no wrong in her son, adding, 'Patrick's character changed as he grew up and he had no father to control him, but he had an independent spirit.'

Brown and Whitlock looked around the house, but except for the chicken carcass — which they overlooked — the only sign that Mackay had been there was a grey Gabardine coat, flecked with blood. The pair then headed to London and made enquiries at Scotland Yard. They found Mackay had previously lived with a Rev Brack, but his address was not listed in the files.

Fearing that Mackay was on a priest-killing spree and the vicar could be his next victim, they made several frantic and unwanted early morning phone calls to a string of London clergymen. Eventually one of them gave the officers an address. They raced to Rev Brack's home in Finchley but the priest was out. Returning thirty minutes later after realizing they had no alternative leads, they found he was safely back home. He couldn't tell them much because he had genuinely not seen Mackay for months, but he could direct them to the hostel in the Great North Road where he believed he was living. The officers ran to the address, but he wasn't there.

Mackay had spent the night on the Cowdreys' sofa, after turning up late at The Clarence pub for a post-murder drink. The Cowdreys later reported that their friend had been more erratic than usual and defensive about his whereabouts that day. As Leigh explained:

> 'Patrick came in sometime after our arrival on his own. I cannot give the exact time he came in but it was near to closing time which is 11pm. Patrick was wearing the same clothing I had seen him wearing the previous night, when we went to the fair. The only unusual thing I noticed was that Patrick had a dark stain on his shirt near the collar. It was only a small spot and I only noticed it when he took his suede coat off. I must admit that I did not pay much attention to Patrick as I was playing darts most of the time. Patrick purchased a few rounds of drinks as usual and we all left the public house together at closing time. Patrick was well drunk at this time and I would have said that he had had a few drinks before he joined us in the Clarence that evening. I never asked him where he'd been that day before he joined us. I don't know how much money he had with him. We arrived home sometime after 11pm and went to bed. Patrick again slept on the couch in the front room.'

Mackay had been able to buy drinks in the pub because he had £6 in his pocket and had lied to the ticket officers at Gravesend Station about being skint. The next morning, just as the detectives arrived at the hostel in the Great North Road, Mackay phoned and the manager Brian Hainey answered. Mackay said he was phoning for a 'chat'. Brown and Whitlock listened but decided not to intervene. Instead, they searched Mackay's room — finding jewellery worth £1,500 — and told the manager to fish for clues to his whereabouts if Mackay should call back. A man in an adjoining room told the officers the killer could be with his friends, the Cowdreys, who lived in the Stockwell area. After some research, Brown and Whitlock came up with another thirty possible addresses. They were by now exhausted and it was late, so they called it a day. All they could do was hope that Mackay would not kill again in the meantime.

Meanwhile, unperturbed by the inevitable manhunt set in motion by killing Father Crean, Mackay had spent the day committing more crimes. Before he left the Cowdreys' home in Stockwell for the day, Bert had caught him standing at the kitchen sink in his underpants, scrubbing the bottom of his trousers with a wire brush. Mackay realized police might be looking for him, so he thought it would be a good idea to change his clothes. After wandering into the Royal Marsden Hospital in Chelsea and stealing a trilby hat, coat, watch and purse from a patient, he went to nearby Callow Street, where he targeted Miriam Durham, whom he spotted walking into her house.

Mackay knocked on her door and asked to use the toilet before forcing his way in. He marched her into the kitchen where he picked up a knife, before declaring: 'This is a knife. I don't use knives.' It was chillingly dishonest. He then demanded food and a cup of tea. He told Miriam he had just been let out of Tooting Bec Hospital, that his name was Hammond and he was from the Newcastle area. Small talk exhausted, he eventually demanded money. Rifling through Miriam's purse, he found she had just £3.

'Is that all you have?' he asked.

'Yes,' she replied.

'Then you'll have to do without it, won't you?' he sneered. Mercifully, he took it and left.

That evening of 22 March, the Cowdrey family again went to the pub and Mackay joined them. Vi would later tell police:

> 'Patrick came into the pub on his own at 9.50pm that evening. He was wearing the same clothing as before, but in addition he had on a large grey overcoat and what appeared to be a suede trilby hat.

95

I later asked him where he had got the additional clothes and he said he had bought them at a market for £10. At some time during that evening, as a result of what I had read in the newspaper, I asked him if he knew anything about the vicar that had been murdered in Kent, meaning had he seen it in the newspaper, and I remember he said, "What do you think I am, fucking mad?" I complained to him about his language, and the evening continued as before.'

Despite the awkward questions, Mackay couldn't help showing off the stolen goods that he had acquired during the day. Later, added Vi, Mackay appeared 'very drunk'.

When they got home, Mackay became hysterical and started screaming at 12-year-old Beverley. 'He shouted, "Shut your mouth or I'll rip the tits off your body,"' recalled Vi. She intervened but he continued to act strangely 'waving his arms and legs about' until she quietened him down and left him in the front room to sleep. He had first got angry at The Clarence, when Terry had picked up Mackay's trilby hat and put it on his own head. 'Terence made some remark like, "This looks like this belongs to a vicar,"' said Vi. Mackay snatched the hat back and threw it onto a window sill.

Later, Terry recalled Mackay's exact words were 'Don't you mention vicars to me. I hate them, I could kill them.'

Earlier that week, Terry added, Mackay had spoken specifically about killing Father Crean. 'I remember quite clearly that he threatened to kill a priest in Kent,' said Terry. 'He said that he hated him and that he was going to smash his face in. He went through the actions of delivering blows and said that he was going to smash his head to bits.'

He used similar violent language when talking to Vi, as she would later tell police: 'At no time has Patrick Mackay ever said to me that he had killed the Father in Kent,' she

Harold, Patrick, Marion and Ruth Mackay at home in the 1950s. Behind the scenes, Harold abused his wife and children.

A young Patrick Mackay playing with stolen gnomes in his garden in Gravesend. Neighbours also noticed him playing with dead birds.

Patrick Mackay aged 10, playing with sand figures of his parents on holiday. He struggled to accept his father's death and would often tell people he was alive.

Above left: Cafe owner Ivy Davies, who was battered to death in her front room. Mackay allegedly said he had thought about robbing her. (*Southend Echo*).

Above right: Police search land close to Ivy's cottage. Although the murder weapon was found in the house, a number of knives were handed in by the public. (*Southend Echo*).

Above left: Detective Chief Inspector Peter Croxford with the pry bar used to kill Ivy Davies. The weapon was found just yards from her body. (*Southend Echo*).

Above right: Detectives examining the door at Ivy's cottage. The killer may have taken the keys with him. (*Southend Echo*).

The team investigating the murder of Ivy Davies. Alf Mitchell is seated second from left, Dave Bright is standing. Around thirty boxes of paperwork were collected. (*Southend Echo*).

Thousands of posters were displayed in Southend following Ivy Davies' murder, but her killer was never found. (*Southend Echo*).

Police standing guard outside the cottage where Ivy Davies was murdered. (*Southend Echo*).

Ivy Davies pictured with her doppelganger Margaret Jewry, mother of pop star Alvin Stardust. (*Southend Echo*).

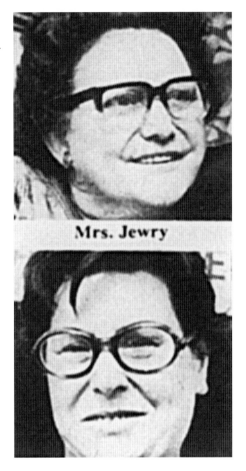

Mrs. Jewry

Patrick Mackay and Leigh Cowdrey feeding birds in Trafalgar Square.

Reverend Ted Brack.
The Anglican curate took
Mackay in but was lucky to
escape with his life.

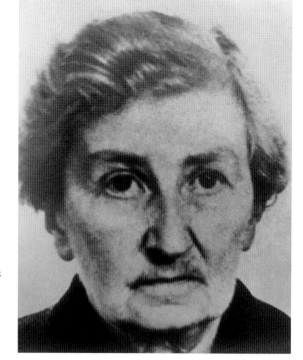

Widow, Isabella Griffiths, was
murdered after a St Valentine's
Day meal with friends.
Mackay had absconded from
a psychiatric hospital the
same day.

Mackay was an arrogant psychopath who planned world domination under the name Franklin Bolvolt the First. He boasted of wanting to 'wipe out' old people.

Adele Price, a widow who was strangled in her flat near Harrods.

Adele Price's sitting room, where her body was found. After killing her, Mackay fell asleep in an armchair. (Metropolitan Police).

Father Anthony Crean. The priest met Mackay while walking in fields near his home – perhaps the killer had engineered the encounter.

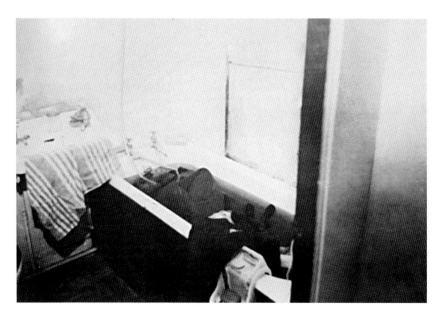

The body of Father Anthony Crean floating in his bathtub. Mackay had draped a towel over his head to hide his injuries. (Kent Police).

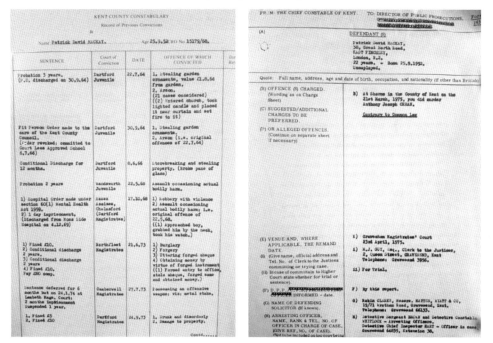

Above left: An extract from Mackay's criminal record shows he was a crook from the age of 11.

Above right: Mackay's charge sheet for the murder of Father Anthony Crean.

Mick Whitfield and Bob Brown, the officers who brought Mackay's reign of terror to an end.

Patrick Mackay. Photobooth self-portrait.

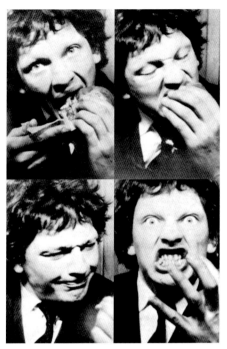

Above left: Portrait of a psychopath. Mackay in a photobooth with chicken he took from his mother's after killing Father Crean.

Above right: A sketch of Mary 'Molly' Hynes. Mackay described stuffing a stocking in her mouth but denied murdering her. (Metropolitan Police).

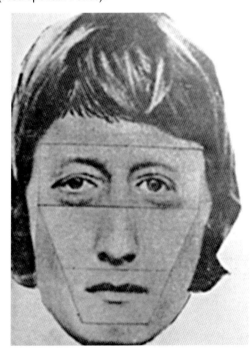

A photofit of a suspect for the murder of Mary Hynes. (Metropolitan Police).

Above left: Frank Goodman. The football fan was battered to death in his sweet shop as the World Cup kicked off. Mackay was charged with murder but the case was left to lie on file.

Above right: Patrick Mackay in his police mugshot. (Metropolitan Police).

Heidi Mnilk. The teenage nanny was stabbed in the neck and thrown from a moving train.

Above left: Photofit of the suspect in the Heidi Mnilk case. (Metropolitan Police).

Above right: A female police officer poses as murder victim Sarah Rodmell. A barman from the Temple Street Tap also took part in the re-enactment. (*Hackney Gazette*).

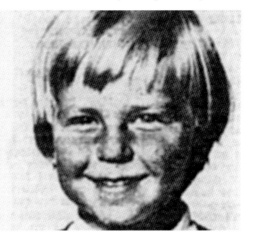

Murder victims Stephanie Britton and her grandson Christopher Martin.

Police frogmen search ponds near Stephanie Britton's home. (*Barnet Press*).

Above left: Blood on Sarah Rodmell's doorstep in East London. The £5 stolen from her purse was a pensioner's Christmas bonus. (*Hackney Gazette*).

Above right: Bert and Vi Cowdrey with the Nazi eagle Mackay kept at their home. He also created a shrine to the fascist party at his mother's home and kept a photo of Himmler by his bed.

Angry MPs demand change in system that let psychopath go on rampage of death

LIFE FOR THE MAD KILLER LAW LET GO

Rates: Read the

Mail says Minister

EVERY ratepayer needs his Daily Mail. Every local ratepayer should pay heed to the Mail's rates campaign.

That was the message yesterday from none other than the Right Hon. Anthony Crosland, Minister of the Environment.

He told a large open Press conference:

> Local authorities now have the choice of either increasing the rates or of reading the Daily Mail every day and cutting out the kind of expenditure which the Mail consistently and very rightly has been attacking.

Mr Crosland called the conference to announce that the Government is to reduce its financial help to town halls.

As the Mail revealed exclusively on Thursday the cutback will amount to £100 million.

Mr Crosland's advice to town hall bosses who are finding it difficult to cut their costs: Read the

Daily Mail

Town halls put on the spot—Page NINE.

Daily Mail Reporters

ANGRY MPs last night demanded a change in the mental health law after mass killer Patrick Mackay was jailed for life at the Old Bailey.

For as psychopath Mackay's horrifying rampage of death and mugging was detailed, it was revealed that, despite his criminal record, he was twice freed from mental hospitals on purely medical decisions.

Doctor warned of risk

Daily Mail Reporter

A TOP psychiatrist yesterday said last night that he twice fought against the release of psychopath Patrick Mackay from a mental hospital.

Each time he was overruled by senior tribunals.

Dr Robert Porter, now 40, was deputy medical superin-

While an urgent Government 'inquest' got under way, 23-year-old Mackay—a man who admitted he enjoyed killing — was under constant guard in the hospital wing of Brixton Prison before transfer to an isolated medical ward at Parkhurst.

Earlier, surrounded in the dock by six burly prison officers, he listened so emotions as he listened to a 60-minute catalogue of his crimes.

Dangerous

The only words he spoke were in answer to the charges, and he echoed them in response to his defence counsel : 'Not guilty to murder . . . guilty to manslaughter on the grounds of diminished responsibility.'

Tall and gaunt, he stood to attention as Mr Justice Milmo said : 'You are a highly dangerous man and it is my duty to protect the public.

'That I can only do by making an order which will ensure that unless and until you cease to be the menace you now are, you will be kept in secure custody.'

PATRICK MACKAY . . . 'Killing is an animal instinct.'

Locals at the Temple Street Tap collecting money for 'Old Sarah's' funeral. The killer was never found. (*Hackney Gazette*).

Vic Davies (left), son of Ivy Davies, with the author. He doesn't think enough has been done to investigate Mackay as a suspect in his mother's murder.

said, but when the police visited the house to ask him about stealing property from Rev Brack, she saw him get angry. 'He became very annoyed about the vicar's allegation. He went almost berserk saying and demonstrating how he was going to see this vicar and smash his head and kill him. I do not think that he was referring to anyone in Kent. This occurrence was at least five or six weeks ago.' Her statement confirmed just how close the kindly Rev Brack had been to becoming another of Mackay's victims.

At 11am the following morning, Mackay stirred, hungover as usual. As he sat talking to Bert Cowdrey there was a knock at the door. It was detectives Brown and Whitlock. By an incredible stroke of luck they had come up trumps with the first address on their list. Bert opened the door and Whitlock saw Mackay standing in the hallway. Whitlock noticed the scratch marks on the back of his right hand.

'We want to speak to you regarding a serious matter but as there are other people present in the house we would like you to come to Clapham Police Station with us in order that we can ask you some questions about your recent movements,' said Whitlock.

'Yes, I will come with you,' Mackay replied calmly.

'Have you anything here that belongs to you, apart from what you stand up in?'

'Only the hat and coat. What's it all about?'

'You know Father Crean, of Shorne?' asked Whitlock. 'He was murdered on Friday and we want to speak to you to see if you know anything about it.'

'Oh, I wondered what it was about,' said Mackay casually.

And with that simple exchange of words on the Cowdreys' doorstep, the world was finally safe from Patrick Mackay. Over the following days and weeks, the softly spoken 22-year-old would stun detectives with a set of gruesome revelations about his many crimes — some of them yet undetected.

Chapter 6

Confessions of a Mad Axeman

Patrick Mackay's killing spree had finally been brought to an end, but it was more by luck than detection. The identity of the prime suspect for the murder of Father Anthony Crean was blindingly obvious from the start and Mackay did not exactly make a great effort to evade capture. He woke up bleary-eyed as usual on the Cowdreys' sofa after another drinking session, with little or no understanding of the consequences of his actions in Kent. When he was tracked down, Mackay went along without a fuss.

Now the young man who had seemingly been able to rob, terrorize and murder at will was in the hands of the police. But although detectives strongly suspected Mackay had carried out the brutal axe murder of Father Crean, they still had to extract a confession. Fortunately, Mackay was keen to open up.

The journey from the Cowdreys' home in Stockwell to Clapham Police Station lasted just a few minutes. Mackay sat in silence, his eyes fixed on the London streets zipping past on the other side of the glass. As he was starting to comprehend that the previous night in The Clarence would be his last real taste of freedom, he was hit by a strange, somewhat alien, sensation. It was soon to become obvious in interviews that he was overcome, not with guilt, but with relief.

While Mackay had never battled his demons in any meaningful sense, he had tried to end his life on several occasions, either by gassing himself in an oven, knifing himself in the chest, hanging or throwing himself under a train. Even if they were not all genuine attempts to die, it was clear that he agonized over the thoughts going on in his head. It is unlikely that the cause of Mackay's anguish was guilt about the people he harmed. As a psychopath, he was incapable of experiencing empathy or remorse. Although he recognized the hurt he inflicted on others and the injustice of his decision to take innocent lives, the murders did not burden him mentally. But he did find his psychological problems frustrating. They left him unable to form meaningful relationships or hold down jobs, and his violent rages meant he was not in control of his own destiny. A day in the life of Patrick Mackay could turn from the mundane to the dramatic in the blink of an eye. It was exhausting and he was unable to understand exactly why he behaved this way.

Now, in the back of a police car with officers Bob Brown and Mick Whitlock, he felt a calmness wash over him. Whatever happened from now on, responsibility for the direction of his life would be turned over to the authorities. Perhaps someone might even be able to fix the problems in his head and he could begin to have a normal existence. Later, Mackay would beg to be sent to Broadmoor Hospital for the criminally insane, home to some of Britain's most notorious criminals, including Peter Sutcliffe, the Yorkshire Ripper. He hoped doctors could cure him and he might one day return to society. This hope was to be extinguished after Mackay's sentencing judge was told psychopathy was not a mental illness but rather a disorder, and therefore not treatable.

Once at the police station Mackay was ushered through the custody lobby and taken immediately to the special constable's room. This was not a television cop show scenario; there was no fanfare or round of applause for the capture of a serial killer. At this point, the identity of the killer of Isabella

Griffiths and Adele Price remained a mystery and, to be blunt, nobody at Clapham nick — down in south-west London and far from the crime scenes — even cared. Police officers, lawyers and fellow detainees shuffled past, oblivious to the monster in their midst. Once in the room, Mackay had one hand cuffed to the desk, but he was allowed to smoke a cigarette. Three cups of tea were rustled up and the trio settled down for a formal interview.

It is worth noting that police interviews were much more relaxed in those days. Mackay had no lawyer present, the interview was not recorded and the transcript was typed up from the officers' handwritten notes. Naturally, the system was open to abuse. Criminals often complained of being 'verballed' — the practice of being made to sign statements containing words they never said. One former detective I spoke to said officers viewed it as 'positive corruption' and it helped them in cases where they might otherwise struggle to convict someone they 'knew' was guilty. Of course, it also led to numerous high-profile miscarriages of justice and the practice was eventually ended, along with the careers of many police officers who engaged in the abuse.

What follows has been pieced together from various transcripts of interviews with Mackay. On some occasions his lawyer was present, on others he was not. But all the accounts given of the interviews by the officers remain consistent and Mackay never challenged the results, so we must accept that the records accurately reflect what was said.

Brown began by cautioning Mackay and asking a few basic questions about the day Father Crean was killed. It was the first and last time he would interview a serial killer, although he didn't know it then. Looking across the desk at Mackay — who had been a model prisoner since his arrest (later Brown would say he found him 'placid and compliant owing to a massive hangover') — he couldn't help but think about the shocking violence meted out to Father Crean, and how the priest had been left floating so horribly in his bathtub. Even in the confines of the police station, with the suspect cuffed to the desk, sitting across from such a violent individual was intimidating. He knew nothing about Mackay's other activities, except the demented incident where he roasted his pet tortoise over a fire, and saw no reason to treat him differently from any other low-life criminal from Gravesend. He certainly wasn't going to pussyfoot around him. It was a matter of pride to secure not only the arrest but the confession, and he knew when they got back to their regular nick a more senior officer would take over.

'This one is mine,' thought Brown and he asked Mackay when he had last visited Gravesend.

'Thursday. No, Friday. It could have been Thursday,' replied Mackay.

'We want you to be sure.'

'It was Friday.'

Mackay told Brown he won a chicken in a raffle at an arcade in Gravesend and persuaded his mum to cook it. After speaking to her about the chicken he went to the cinema, then went home and ate most of the chicken before leaving Gravesend about 7.15pm. Brown immediately picked a hole in his story.

'Your mum says she hasn't seen you since the new year. Why would she say that?'

'I don't know.'

'You definitely saw your mum when you went home?'

'Yes, she cooked the chicken.'

'Look, you know why we're asking these questions,' said Brown. 'We've already told you. I put it to you that you went to Father Crean's and killed him.'

If Mackay had stuck to his story, perhaps under the advice of a solicitor, the case would probably have gone to trial. After all, nobody had seen him at Father Crean's cottage, although a resident of Shorne did later give a statement about a man knocking at his door asking for water and directions after the killing had taken place. The witness may or may not have positively identified Mackay. Police would have needed to prove Mackay wielded the axe, and because his gloved hands left no forensic evidence behind, that could have been tricky. It is then perhaps a little surprising that Mackay caved in so quickly. He barely paused before he gave his blunt reply: 'Yes, I did. I thought you'd get me.'

Perhaps he was overwhelmed by impulse, which is the hallmark of a psychopath. Perhaps he feared the case against him would be too strong. Notwithstanding the lack of witnesses and forensics left at the scene, he had made a string of incriminating comments to the Cowdreys, already lied about his time spent in Gravesend, and there was blood on his clothes. There was also the matter of his notoriously fractious relationship with the priest. The strong circumstantial evidence would weigh heavily against him at a trial. Whatever the reason, Brown could hardly believe his luck. Mackay had admitted the most serious of offences within minutes of light questioning.

'I will remind you again that you have been cautioned,' he warned. 'Would you like to tell us about it?'

'I owed him some money, about £30,' lied Mackay, barely skipping a beat. 'I went in there and told him I was the man who did him for the money. A little dog ran off. I've got a lot more to tell you. When I first went in there he wasn't there. Then he came in and shouted "Oh, my God!" He ran. I just saw clouds. It was just like a white mist.'

'What did you hit him with?' asked Brown.

'When I looked at him again, I wasn't looking at a man,' responded Mackay. 'I was looking at a mess.'

'Can you tell us what you hit him with?'

'I don't know. It was like a mist.'

Brown continued to probe. He was concerned that when interviewed later with his lawyer present, Mackay might change his story. If he mentioned details now that only the killer could have known, it would help ensure the case was watertight.

'What were you wearing when you did it?' he asked.

'What I had on this morning, except that hat and coat.'

'Try and remember what you hit him with.'

'It might have been a knife. I had two.'

'Where are they now?'

'I threw one away near here. I can't remember where the other one is. I haven't got it now.'

'Where's the knife that you threw away? Can you point out where you threw it?'

'Yes, it's on a roof. I threw it over a wall. I don't think I used it on Father Crean.'

Brown paused. Mackay seemed confused. Although the officer knew some of what he was saying was true, he could also be telling lies. He wondered if Mackay was genuinely confused or pretending. He wanted to make sure he was eliciting a true confession.

'How did you get those scratches on your hand?'

'They're from an old fight at a fair I went to.'

'Were you wearing these gloves when you attacked Father Crean?' Brown held up a pair of kid gloves that had been in Mackay's coat pocket.

'Yes.'

'What was Father Crean wearing?'

'A suit I think.'

'Anything else that you noticed?'

'Grey socks. Yes, definitely grey socks.'

'How do you know that?'

'One of his boots came off.' That much was true.

Brown ended the interview at 1.30pm and left the room to arrange transport to Northfleet Police Station in Kent. He had obtained an initial confession, albeit without Mackay's solicitor in attendance. But that didn't really matter to him.

There was no way this was going to trial. Now it would be up to more senior officers to charge Mackay on home turf and extract further details. Officer Whitlock stayed in the room while Brown left to make the call. But Mackay had not finished talking.

'Do you believe that each person has individual destiny?' he asked Whitlock.

'In some circumstances it often appears that way,' he replied, bemused by the question.

'This is certainly mine,' said Mackay, lighting another cigarette. 'This situation had to happen.'

* * *

Before heading back to Kent, Mackay showed the officers an address in Clapham Road where he said he threw one of the knives used in the attack on Father Crean onto a roof. By 4pm, all three were at Northfleet Police Station. Brown's eagerness to secure the initial confession before senior officers muscled in was quickly vindicated; Mackay was turned over to DI Lewis Hart in a matter of minutes. In his second interview, the young psychopath was much more forthcoming, revealing a level of callousness that surprised even the veteran detectives.

'In January I was here,' Mackay told Hart. 'I had a barney with my mother and didn't come down for about three weeks. I then made a few visits. Just days, not staying overnight. We had another barney and I hadn't been back again until this Friday.'

'You came back on Friday and made up the barney with your family?' asked Hart sounding sympathetic. His questions were soft and his tone understanding. He knew Mackay had a violent temper and could be a tricky customer but Brown and Whitlock had briefed him on his arrest and the initial interview. They had all taken the softly-softly approach and so far it appeared to be working.

'Yes, and to explain to Father Crean about the money that I owe him. I did that once before,' replied Mackay.

'You went to his house before?' asked Hart. 'When was this?'

'About six months after I went to court about the cheque I stole from him. I went to explain that he would get his money back and made some arrangements about it with him. He wasn't in that time at first.' Mackay was talking about the occasion when Father Crean said he wanted no more to do with him before driving off. 'I think he thought I was being a bit of a pest.'

'Why did you decide to go there on this occasion?' asked Hart.

'I had it in my mind to visit him again and explain to him why I hadn't paid any money.'

'Where did you make up your mind to come down?'

'At Terry Cowdrey's house. I made an excuse to them by saying that I was going down to the country to do some tree cutting. I just made up the story so that it would be alright for me to go back there and stay if I wanted. I didn't want them to think I was just using them. I had intention of moving back down here, but I said that rather than saying I was leaving.'

Mackay revealed that before travelling to Kent he visited Vauxhall Library to borrow a book, *If Britain Had Fallen*, by Norman Longmate. It explored the Nazis real-life plans to occupy Britain and what could have happened if they'd been successful.

Mackay told DI Hart that he got to Gravesend about 1.30pm, hanging around first at an arcade and then winning the chicken in a raffle. As Hart pushed him on the details of the afternoon, Mackay switched between being unsure of exactly how events unfolded to being crystal clear. One thing was certain — he was willing to admit that he had been to Father Crean's cottage and he was chillingly matter of fact about the violence he unleashed there.

He described his route to the cottage along Thong Lane, past the primary school and towards the church and that he noticed Father Crean's blue Volkswagen outside and smoke rising from the garden.

'I knew he did a lot of gardening so I wondered if he was out there. I couldn't see him,' he said.

'What did you do then?' asked Hart.

'I pushed the front door open and called out, "Mr Crean are you there?" There was no answer. I walked in a little way and knocked the white door that leads to his sitting room.'

'Is that on the right or the left?'

'To the left. It was locked.'

'Did you knock?'

'Yes. I turned the handle, it was locked, I thought I would wait.'

'Where did you wait?'

'Where he keeps his bike in that hallway under the stairs. There was a pair of boots there too.'

'While you waited did you sit or stand?'

'I stood there.'

'How long do you think you stood there?'

'About five minutes. I should have stayed outside shouldn't I?' asked Mackay calmly.

'You are very bad at recalling times aren't you?' asked Hart, changing tack.

'Yes, I am. If things are urgent I normally remember okay. Or if I have to be somewhere at a certain time.'

'Did you look around the house while you waited?'

'Yes, I waited about then went up his stairs and looked in a bedroom and called out for him.'

'Was there anything in the bedroom?'

'No, it looked like a guest room, all neat and tidy. The bed had a red cover on. It didn't look like anyone was using the room.'

'You came downstairs then?'

'Yes, I went in his bedroom then and saw some clerical clothes there.'

'Was this upstairs?'

'No, downstairs. I had a look around. I remember the fridge, looking in the fridge.'

'Why the fridge? Why look in there? Were you hungry?'

'No, I always look in fridges.' For the first time, Mackay alluded to other crimes. Hart made a note of the comment but decided to keep the interview focused on the events at the cottage. There would be plenty of time to discuss further offences later. He was sure of that.

'A lot of people keep money in fridges,' said Hart. 'Were you looking for money?'

'No, I saw a safe there that was locked. I was in a downstairs bedroom when I heard him come in.'

'Did you look around to see what you could take?'

'No. The exact truth is that wasn't my original intention, to go there to steal anything. I saw the stuff about but I didn't take anything.'

Hart didn't believe him. 'I can't find a cheque book that should be there. Did you take that?'

'No, no cheque book.'

'Did you take any money?'

'No, none at all.'

DS Brown chipped in, asking about items police had found on his person, including a watch and a miniature sword. Both were stolen the day after the killing. Mackay said he bought the watch and didn't steal the sword. He then altered his story and said he was looking in the fridge for a can of beer, and wasn't in the bedroom when Father Crean came home.

'I heard a noise, a scraping, juddering noise, the front door opening,' he said. 'Father Crean came in. He didn't see me, he had his back to me. He was opening the white door with the key. He walked through the white door and into the sitting room. He still hadn't seen me, he turned back towards me.

He was bending, looking down, lighting his pipe. He still hadn't seen me. I said "Mr Crean." He looked up and said "Good God" and something else.'

'How long did you stand before you approached him?' asked Hart.

'He came towards me into the doorway.'

'He stood still there?'

'Yes, I had moved from the bedroom towards him before he looked up, just a short distance before I spoke.'

'How far away were you when he looked up?'

'Just arm's length. He tried to run for the door, I grabbed him. I wanted to explain what I was doing there. He said something about the police being on the way. He said, "Don't go for me, don't be stupid," or something.'

'You say you grabbed him?'

'Yes,' replied Mackay.

Hart asked if he'd seen a dog. The whereabouts of Father Crean's beloved Jacko were important for the purposes of establishing a timeline. Mackay said it had run past his legs and out the door when he'd entered the house.

'When the Father came back did the dog come back with him?' asked Hart.

'I don't know.'

'What did he say exactly when he had first seen you and tried to run out?'

'Something about police or people on their way. That's when I grabbed him. I tried to explain about returning money. It all then seemed very strange, all seemed misty.'

'Try and think clearly,' instructed Hart. 'You did this with something. What was it? Where did it come from?'

'He had some tools, metal bars and some shears by the stairs. I might have used the shears and smashed him.'

'What was it you used? I know you can tell me. What was it? Where did you put it afterwards? Think.'

'There was a saw,' said Mackay. 'We were rolling and struggling on the floor.'

'That's right,' agreed Hart. 'There was a saw by the stairs. There were other tools by the stairs as well.' Like Brown in the first interview, Hart needed to make sure Mackay could give a full and accurate account of what happened. At the same time, it was clear that Mackay's memory was fuzzy — or that he wanted it to appear that way. Hart kept pressing, certain that Mackay would remember — or admit to — the precise details.

'Yes,' said Mackay. 'In the hallway, where you go towards where his bike was, where we were rolling about. I remember he stretched out towards the shears, or he might have been trying to get his pipe, which dropped on the floor when we were struggling, I hit him with my hands.'

'I know what it was you used,' said Hart gently. 'But I want you to tell me.'

'I know I used a weapon,' said Mackay. 'I saw him afterwards. Just a mess.'

'Try to think what it was,' pressed Hart.

'It might have been a hammer or an axe,' said Mackay. 'That's right. I remember, it was an axe. I had it in my hand afterwards.'

Mackay had placed himself at the scene, with the murder weapon, at exactly the right time for Father Crean's murder. But Hart needed him to go further. It was vital that no detail was left out, because Mackay could still plead not guilty in court later on. In that case there would be a trial and if Mackay had a clever barrister, he could try and wriggle out of it. But even Hart, a seasoned detective wasn't prepared for the callousness that followed. The motive, Mackay said, was simple: he was 'annoyed'.

'When did you pick the axe up?' asked Hart. 'Before the Father came back to the house?'

'No, it was during the struggle I picked it up.'

'Then what?'

'I smashed it down.'

'Where?'

'On his head or something.'

'Where did this happen? What part of the house did you go to?'

'Quite possibly to the bathroom,' answered Mackay.

'How was it that you left the stairs area and got to the bathroom?'

'When he first saw me, he tried to run out. I grabbed his arm, we struggled and fell on the floor. We struggled on the floor, he got away and I was annoyed because I wanted to explain about the money. He wouldn't listen, I went for the axe. He said, "Don't hurt me." I got annoyed.'

'What state were you in when you went to get the axe?'

'I felt like doing it,' said Mackay simply.

'Why go for the axe if you just wanted to explain?'

'I got annoyed because he was excitable and wouldn't listen.'

'What were you intending to do at that stage with the axe?'

'I seemed to want to tell him not to force me to use it. I wanted him to be quiet. I just got the urge to use it.'

'For what?'

'To take his head off.' Mackay raised his voice and it was clear he was becoming agitated. Hart knew he had to keep pushing.

'What happened?' he asked.

'As I said, he got away and I got the axe. He went in the bathroom and tried to close the door.'

'He tried to close the bathroom door?'

'Yes, I pushed it open and pushed him. He fell partially into the bath, I put the axe down then and pushed him all the way into the bath.'

'Which end of the bath was his head when you pushed him in the bath?'

'Originally he was with his head towards the window, but I pulled him around and hit him with my gloved hands.'

'Did you wear gloves all the time?'

'When I first went in, then I took them off and put them back on when I was waiting for him to come in.'

'What position was he in after you had pulled him around?'

'His head was towards the door then.'

'Was he saying anything to you at that time?'

'No, I was lashing him with my arm, like that.' Mackay demonstrated hitting the priest with his fists. There was fury in his face and hatred in his eyes. 'It all took such a short time,' he said.

'Was he bleeding then?' asked Hart.

'Yes. His face, his nose where I hit him it bled. It seemed his eye went black as I hit him. The blood made me excited, made me worse.'

'What position was his head?'

'Towards the door end of the bath.'

'What level was his head when you were hitting him?'

'He was sitting up in the bath then.'

'Is that when you picked up the axe?'

'I picked up the axe, I used...', Mackay looked confused. 'Hang on a second, I used the knife. That one I told them to get might not be that one though. I threw away two knives.'

'Were they your knives?'

'Yes, I always carry two knives for protection. You know there are a lot of people around these days, violent and that.' Hart wasn't sure whether this was Mackay's attempt at self-effacing humour. If it was, there was no hint in his eyes. He seemed oblivious to the magnitude of his crime. The violence he had used was so out of the ordinary, it was the most extreme case Hart had ever dealt with.

'One of these knives is the one that you told Mr Brown about and showed him where to find it?' asked Hart.

'Yes, that was one of them.'

'So, you pulled out one of these knives before you picked up the axe again?'

'Yes, I lunged at his throat lots of times, sticking and sticking and sticking it. He was making noises, like gurgling from his throat, then I hit him in the temple with it. It went in right up to the hilt then I tried to stab him in the top of his head. I banged away but it just buckled the knife up, really bent it. When I got him in the side of the head he put his hand up and he slid down the bath making a long, long, long noise, I suppose it was the noise you make…the human body is a funny thing, the anatomy.'

Hart shuddered. Was Mackay playing games? He seemed to flit from recalling the smallest of details to blaming the 'mist' for failing to remember his more significant actions. Could it be possible that Mackay was setting up a defence for himself; not just for the murder of Father Crean but for other crimes he'd already hinted at committing? If he was later questioned about offences for which there was less clear-cut evidence, he could point to his behaviour during this first interview and claim he was consistently poor at remembering events.

'What did you do with the knife then?' asked Hart.

'I threw it on the floor and picked up the axe, then struck him with it on the head a few times and around the temple. That exposed his brain.'

'How do you know that it was his brain?' pressed Hart. 'What colour was it?'

'It was his brain alright, like wriggles, grey and white.'

'Is that when you stopped hitting him?'

'Yes.'

'Then what?'

'I ripped the plug out of the sink and put it in the bath and filled it up.'

'Did you notice anything on the taps?'

'No, they were just ordinary taps. He was making noises, his face was washed with the water.'

'Did you leave the taps on?'

'I think I did. I may have turned them off. I can't remember really.'

'Why did you turn the taps on?'

'Because I didn't like the blood, but the water turned crimson.'

For the first time in the interview, Mackay had shown some basic humanity. He was squeamish, and perhaps a little ashamed of the scene he had created in Father Crean's bathroom.

'I picked up the axe again and threw it back in the toolbox under the stairs. I went back to the bathroom and stayed there looking at him for about an hour. I opened the window and looked at the sky for a while.' 'Why did you stay there?' asked Hart.

'I don't know. It's strange, I just felt I wanted to.'

'What did you do with the knife?'

'I put it back in my pocket.'

'How did you leave the house eventually?'

'I went out the front door and walked around outside in the garden for a while. I remember the grass was muddy. I kept picking up dirt and mud and things. I don't know why, just doodling about really. I went back indoors and stayed looking at him again.'

'When you walked out of the house how far did you go?'

'Not far, just around the house in a semicircle and then back in.'

'You stayed there about an hour afterwards you say?'

'Yes, I got a bit puzzled about the dog. I wondered if I had slaughtered that as well.'

The response stunned Hart. 'You don't know to this day what happened about the dog then?'

'No.'

Mackay described leaving the cottage, knocking on a villager's door for a glass of water and walking past a police car. 'It didn't worry me much,' he said. He added that when he got back to his mother's house 'she said a funny thing. She said, "Where have you been? Burying a body in the woods?" It was just a joke, I suppose coincidence. I washed my hands to get the mud off.'

'Did you have any blood on your hands?' asked Hart.

'No, that all washed off in the bath water.'

Mackay then confessed to an act that he would repeat in at least one other murder. He told Hart that Father Crean was a 'mess' and he put a 'piece of cloth' (a towel) over his head.

'Why did you do that?'

'Because of the wounds and blood on his head. They didn't look very nice.'

'Did you put any lights on or touch the curtains in the cottage?' asked Hart.

'I put lights on in the front room and the bathroom, in fact all the lights I think. I don't think I drew the curtains though. I'm not sure but I might well have done, yes.'

'Are you a Roman Catholic?' asked Hart.

'No, definitely not.'

'Did you see the priest with anything in his hands at any time?'

'No, I remember him trying to pick up his pipe as we struggled on the floor.'

'Do you know what a rosary is?'

'Yes, beads and things.'

'Yes. Did you see one at any time while you were at the cottage?'

'No, I didn't.' This was hardly believable. The rosary was found draped over Father Crean's hand and Mackay had admitted to staring at his corpse for more than an hour.

* * *

The interview was paused at 5.25pm. When it restarted, Mackay told the officers about going back to his mother's house after the killing, how she gave him the chicken to take away and that he had watched the Charles Bronson film at the cinema. He described his conundrum at the train station when he realized he had no money left.

He said that when he got to London, he threw one of the knives off Hungerford Bridge into the River Thames and again denied taking anything from Father Crean's cottage. He didn't return to the hostel in the Great North Road because he owed a lot of money. As a result of the debt, he said, he had not been able to change his clothes for weeks. Forensics officers took a sample of blood and hair. Then, Mackay made a full confession, detailing all his movements that day including the murder, which he dictated to Sergeant Brown. He concluded it by saying: 'The only thing I want to add is it didn't seem to trouble me too much what I had done on hearing it in the paper. Apart from that I don't think there is anything more I can put to the statement. I have read the above statement and I have been told that I can correct, alter or add anything I wish. This statement is true. I have made it of my own free will.'

As Sergeant Brown completed the statement, Mackay added, 'I knew this would happen one day. If it hadn't been Father Crean it would have been somebody else.'

'What do you mean?' asked Hart.

'I've felt it in me for a long time. I'm not surprised I've done it. It might even have been me I done it to,' he replied cryptically.

Hart asked about the marks on Mackay's hands. They had bothered him all afternoon because he knew Father Crean had done little to defend himself.

'How did you get those marks on your hands? Roll up your sleeves,' he demanded.

'I had a bit of aggro at a fair at Stockwell last week and got those in a fight,' explained Mackay.

'Who was the fight with?'

'I don't know. We all ran away when the law came.'

'Some of those marks look quite fresh. Did Father Crean cause any of those in the struggle?'

'Yes, this one,' said Mackay offering the back of his right hand. 'And these.' He pointed to parallel marks on his left forearm. The wounds were photographed and at five minutes to midnight, Mackay was charged with murder. 'That's right,' he said when the charge was read out.

Four days later Mackay asked to amend his statement. He had lied to the officers, he said, but not about Father Crean being his first and only victim. He said contrary to what he'd declared in his statement, he didn't win the chicken in a raffle, he stole it from a Tesco in Gravesend. He also claimed he hadn't, as he had said, stolen a hat and coat from the Royal Marsden Hospital, he'd taken them from the Arts Institute, a drama school in the West End. In another amended statement, he admitted lying to the Gravesend ticket officers about not having enough money.

Over the following months, Mackay's propensity to tell lies about anything from minor theft to murder would confuse detectives even as he confessed to a litany of shocking crimes. In his final report on the case, Hart called Mackay 'an inveterate liar', adding, 'He lies even when it is unnecessary about trivial matters. Telling lies is part of his way of life.'

Hart was convinced Mackay had gone to the cottage with the intent to steal, not to repay money. He also suspected Mackay of being behind the two murders and dozens of robberies in the West End. There was a good reason for this — Mackay had lied about the jewellery found in his room at the hostel, saying it was from a burglary carried out at St Martin-in-the-Fields near Trafalgar Square, when in fact the true owner, who lived in Belgravia, had already been traced. And although the grey Gabardine coat found at his mother's house was not the one he wore while killing Father Crean, his explanation for how it got stained with blood was hardly believable. 'I don't remember,' he said. 'It's got me puzzled. I think it's months old, the bloodstain. I cut myself. I don't remember what with.'

But at least the doctors had been right — Patrick Mackay was a cold psychopathic killer. And as detectives delved deeper into his past they started to believe he might even be the most dangerous man in Britain.

Chapter 7

A Strong Compulsion to Kill

The London crime squad tasked with finding the robber of old ladies had stopped placing red dots on its map of the West End. Each of the thirty plus marks represented a targeted attack against an elderly victim, usually in their own home. Two of the dots related to murders; those of Isabella Griffiths and Adele Price. Now the robberies had stopped. The team's boss, DSUP John Bland, had been frustrated with the lack of progress in the investigation. But when Father Anthony Crean was hacked to death twelve days after Adele Price's murder, just a few miles down the road in Kent, Bland's interest was piqued by the news that a Londoner was being questioned over that outrage.

After several months, his squad had little else to go on. Descriptions given by the robber's terrified, elderly victims rarely seemed to match. He would strike at different times of day, making it difficult for plain clothes officers scouring the streets of London's upmarket districts to run into him. And despite clues about treatment he may have received at psychiatric hospitals, Bland had been unable to pinpoint a suspect. But that was about to change.

At a time when forensic science was still in its relative infancy and was yet to imprint itself on the public consciousness through television shows and paperback thrillers, criminals could often afford to be careless at crime scenes. Mackay certainly gave little thought to covering his tracks. His idea of disposing of evidence was to chuck the murder weapon into a river or onto the roof of the nearest building — if he even remembered it was still on him.

He gave even less thought to covering up his involvement in the crimes where he didn't go on to kill. A prime example was the robbery he carried out on 15 February 1975, after forcing his way into the Chelsea home of 79-year-old widow Margaret Diver. She endured a bizarre, hour-long ordeal, during which Mackay veered between chatting amiably and making threats, while drinking tea in her kitchen. As he absent-mindedly stirred the cup, he thought nothing of the incriminating fingerprints he was leaving on the teaspoon.

Bland sent the prints away for forensic analysis, but it was a case of wait and see. Over the following weeks — during which time Mackay killed Father Crean — poor old Adele Price was rarely out of his thoughts. By 6 April, Mackay had been in custody for nearly two weeks. Even though Bland strongly suspected he was their killer, Metropolitan Police issued a new witness appeal warning pensioners about the serial mugger. But six days later the teaspoon print turned up a match: Patrick David Mackay. He was being held on remand at Brixton Prison and Bland immediately requested his transfer to a police station for questioning.

Four days later Mackay was roused from his cell early in the morning, given the opportunity to wash and eat and then escorted to a prison van. He was soon back in familiar surroundings at Northfleet Police Station in Kent. It was the first of many sojourns Mackay would enjoy outside of the prison gates, making him the envy of some of the stir-crazy inmates. Within a couple of hours he was smoking cigarettes and drinking tea with John Bland, DS Derek Ramsay, and DCI David Gerring, who would later become famous for his life-long investigation into the Lord Lucan case.

Mackay had an idea of what they planned to ask him and may have thought about keeping quiet. After all, the police knew about just one killing so far. When questioned on the others, he still had the option of denying the allegations. Otherwise he could simply say he was insane. With psychiatric treatment, he could even be out in a few years.

But in an echo of the first interview about the killing of Father Crean, it took Bland just moments to get a confession. The detective had cut straight to the point. He told Mackay he wanted to talk about the murder of Adele Price in Lowndes Square.

'Yes, I did that,' he replied.

Bland was stunned. His team had spent months toiling in vain to find the robber and killer of old ladies. Now they had him, not just for the robberies but also for the murder of Adele Price. But Bland wanted to be absolutely certain that Mackay was telling the truth, and not simply a troubled young man willing to admit to any crime put before him.

'Could you tell me how you got into her flat?' he asked.

'Yes, I saw her go to her flat, the front door of the house, and let herself in. I pretended I had got keys to get in the house as well, so I walked in with her. I went up the stairs and then pretended I'd got cramp or something in my leg and she invited me in her flat for a cup of tea or glass of water.'

'Where did you murder the woman and how?'

'I put my hand around her neck. It was in the bedroom.'

The confession was quick and easy. Next, Bland asked about the murder of Isabella Griffiths. He believed she had been Mackay's first victim, back in February 1974, and he wanted to strike while the iron was hot. If he could elicit confessions to both murders it would be one of the proudest moments of his career and a long-awaited victory for his robbery squad.

'You mean the Cheyne Walk murder?' asked Mackay.

'What do you know about that?'

'I did it,' he said bluntly. Again, Bland was surprised. It was too easy. Like officers Brown and Hart before him, he knew he must press for all the details to secure Mackay's conviction. And more than that — the sentencing judge would need to know the full extent of Mackay's criminality to give the prosecuting authorities the best chance of having him locked up for the rest of his life. Fortunately, over the following hours, Mackay would insist that his crimes weighed heavily on his conscience and he wanted to make things right and 'clear up' his past.

'What was the woman's name?' asked Bland.

'I don't remember.'

'How did you kill her and where?'

'I went to her home to see if she wanted anything done because I used to run errands for her.'

'What kind of errands?'

'I used to go to the shops and get tins and tins of cat food. She said she didn't want any errands that night and tried to shut the door on me, so I pushed it open.'

'Just pushed it open? As easy as that?'

'No, she had the chain on the door, but I didn't have to give it a very hard push to break it. In the hallway I put my hands around her neck and I later stuck the carving knife in her. I think she was still alive when I did this.'

'Where did you leave her?'

'In the kitchen.'

'Is there anything about the killing of this woman that springs to your mind on this occasion?'

'Yes, at one time her false teeth fell out.'

'Was there anything else?'

'Yes, I seemed to stop at the house for quite some time. I think I was just wandering about the house and listening to the radio. I know at one time I turned the tap on in the kitchen sink and threw everything to hand in. I don't know what made me do this.'

In the same way that Mackay had 'doodled' in the aftermath of Father Crean's murder, he spent considerable time in Isabella Griffiths' home, filling the sink with various items, including her shoes. This had been noted in the statement from Isabella's friend, Eleanor Farquhar. Mackay had also run a tap immediately after slaying the priest, although that had been in the bath, and he sat and watched his victim 'floating about' in the crimson water.

'I've been thinking about these things and when I was told you wanted to see me this morning I guessed what it was about,' said Mackay. 'I have seen the posters up about the old woman in Belgravia and I knew I had done it.'

Bland suggested that whoever killed Adele Price also committed a huge number of robberies in the Chelsea, Knightsbridge and Belgravia areas. Mackay admitted he had 'bag snatched' and said he would confess to any crime he could remember committing. He said he felt some guilt about the robberies:

> 'After I strangled the old woman I tried to do away with myself down the tube and they put me into hospital for a couple of days and when I came out I did three or four in one week. It became like a disease.
>
> 'The one I remember was a nice old lady. We had quite a nice conversation together. She was something to do with the hospital and she tried to get me to go to hospital but I wouldn't. She made me a cup of tea and gave me a sandwich and I remember when I took the money from her I had her name and address, because I gave her some baloney about sending it back to her. I never meant to hurt this woman although at one time I did show her a knife so that she could see that she couldn't mess about with me.'

That woman was Margaret Diver, on whose teaspoon he so helpfully left a fingerprint. He had no idea Bland had already tied him to that crime via the print, and Bland saw no reason to tell him now. Blown away by his confessions, the detectives

121

paused the interview and stepped outside. They decided it would be best to get Mackay to make a written statement as soon as possible, in case the infamous 'mist' — which Mackay liked to cite when he was struggling to recall events — came down again and he 'forgot' the details. But when the officers returned to the interview room Mackay shocked them further by admitting to a fourth, previously undetected, murder.

'All I want is to be frank and honest,' he told them, asking DS Ramsay to take down his statement. 'But before I start I have got another murder I want to get off my mind. The only trouble is I don't know whether the person drowned or not.'

'What was it about?' asked Bland trying to remain calm despite the magnitude of the event. Four murders would make Mackay one of London's most prolific serial killers — almost on a par with Jack the Ripper. Having established that Mackay was responsible for the deaths of a priest and two old women, and now perhaps a fourth person, Bland wondered if he'd even scratched the surface.

'I threw a vagrant off Hungerford Bridge at Waterloo and I saw the water open up and take him in,' said Mackay. It sounded as though he was describing a dream or distant memory; a detached comment delivered with the trademark indifference of a psychopath. 'I don't think he could swim because of him splashing around. I'm sorry to be so much trouble to you. I will tell you all I can remember, but what happens at times is that a curtain comes down over my mind about some of these incidents. This is usually when they are too horrific to remember. I know I've done murders but I just can't remember them when this curtain comes down.'

This comment about having 'done murders' could have been crucial if detectives had later decided to test additional allegations in court. Mackay had already confessed to killing Father Crean, Isabella Griffiths and Adele Price, as well as the unnamed homeless man, and he remembered them clearly. What else could he have been referring to?

Bland took the decision to move Mackay to Canon Row Police Station, part of the New Scotland Yard estate, in order to make the written statement. Once there, Bland went back to the Isabella Griffiths killing. Mackay described how he met the old lady in January 1974, during one of his many boozy rambles around the West End. She had been carrying two heavy bags across Albert Bridge. A perfect target. Mackay offered to carry them home and she invited him in for a glass of his favourite tipple — scotch. He said he went back on several occasions to run errands in return for a small amount of cash. He must have been charming and plausible, although he failed to explain why he chose not to rob or attack her for such a long time. Perhaps he was fighting his urge to kill. A spell in a psychiatric hospital would send him over the edge:

> 'Around this time — I don't remember the dates —
> I got stopped in Stockwell down the tube. Two
> police officers came to arrest me but had to get
> help to stop me throwing myself onto the lines
> and I got sent into Tooting Bec psychiatric unit for
> observation. Whilst I was there they asked me if
> I would like to go for a walk in the grounds and
> I agreed to go and I used this for an excuse to
> leave the hospital. I never heard any more from
> the hospital. It was around this time, but I cannot
> remember if it was before or after Tooting Bec, that
> I returned to the lady's house in Cheyne Walk.'

Mackay killed Isabella Griffiths on St Valentine's Day, 1974, just hours after strolling out of the hospital. He described what happened next in chilling detail:

> 'I got to the door, knocked on the door about
> evening time, because I remember as I walked past
> the house I saw the light on in one of the rooms and
> saw her sitting there. She answered the door but

with the safety chain on. At first she didn't seem to recognize me, then she did and said, "I don't need any shopping done today." I asked her then if she wanted anything done in the house, especially upstairs as she never seemed to venture up there. She said, "No, no. Nobody's going up there." I struck the door and the chain snapped. I gained entry and she backed along the passageway.

'I realized that I had done something I shouldn't have done and I went a bit frantic. The next thing I knew she was on the floor. I had grabbed her around the neck. This was in the kitchen area. I must have pressed her neck hard with my left hand because she went unconscious. Just going down to the kitchen, you remember there was one or two steps leading down to the kitchen, it was a scullery more or less. She lay down the stairs with her head towards the kitchen. I decided then there was still hope yet that she was alive so lay her flat in a better position on the kitchen floor. She was unconscious because she was still breathing. I left her then and ventured into her front room. She already had the wireless on. I listened to a news bulletin on the radio and felt a strong wanting to venture up the stairs. I wandered all up the stairs. There were some rooms that were locked that I could not go into. I entered other rooms that were unlocked and well-furnished but covered in cobwebs and dust. They couldn't have been used for years.

'I then went back down the stairs and had a strong compulsion to kill her outright. For this purpose I picked up a knife for cutting meat, a standard kitchen knife about the length of a twelve-inch ruler in the blade. I then rammed this through her solar plexus, the bone of her chest, dead centre or just a bit below. I felt it embed itself into the floor.

'I then left her there and sat down in the front room and produced a bottle of scotch from my pocket. I emptied it. It did not make me drunk but made me inflamed, you know how whisky warms you up. It rather stimulated me. I listened to [Edward] Heath on the radio, it was the prime minister's speech or something. It must have been something of interest because I stayed to listen to it. I felt sure it was something to do with the Common Market but after all this time I can't be positive. I seemed to forget the fact that someone was lying dead in the kitchen. After the speech was finished I either switched the radio off or down. I then had an extremely uncanny feeling that there was some other presence in the house. By that I mean another person who did not want to be seen. She had spoken to me at some stage of having lodgers. I saw nothing to indicate this. I felt this would rather be a man rather than a woman and may be in the cellar. [Mackay was most probably referring to Hedgegus, the handyman who had left some weeks earlier.]

'I looked for a light switch but couldn't find any, so focused myself to the darkness and went down there. On a door to my left, as I opened it, I saw the room to be full of cats of various descriptions. Two Siamese cats and other breeds. One darted out. One of the other cats came up and sniffed at me. I think I closed the door again.

'I didn't really want them running all over the place. I went back up the stairs, went into the front room and I think got some clothes from there or from the downstairs front room, again I can't be sure. I took these clothes into the kitchen, extracted the knife from the body and straightened the arms into the cross position, something like an

125

undertaker might have done it. I also closed her eyes. I then draped the clothes I had taken from another room over her body, tucking them in at the sides.'

Having recalled that Eleanor Farquhar described the pose as 'beautiful', Bland interrupted Mackay: 'Earlier when talking about this you told me about her false teeth falling out, when did this happen?'

'I think it was the bottom part but it may have been the top part because some people only have a top plate,' responded Mackay. 'This happened when I first grabbed her throat in the hall. They then dropped out. They fell onto the floor and I pushed them with my foot under a small cabinet in the hall. I went into the front room and there was a low sort of a cupboard with the door half open. I saw that this contained bottles of spirits. I closed the door back again. Just before I went out of the house I closed the kitchen door or locked it. This I can't be sure of but I know the door was closed tight.'

Bland asked about the knife. Mackay confessed he thought about committing suicide with it, but chickened out. 'After I had taken the knife out of her body and covered her up, I had a good look at the blade,' he said. 'I contemplated ramming it into my own body but then felt that this was not the thing to do at the present moment. There was a small canvas bag or something of similar material on the table in the front room. I feel sure I put the knife in this. I then made an exit out onto the street taking the knife with me in the bag.'

His fatal attack on Isabella Griffiths had been nasty, brutish and over in moments. It was also apparently of little consequence to Mackay. In fact, he rather enjoyed relaxing in the afterglow; listening to a speech by the prime minister on the radio and exploring the parts of the house that had hitherto been denied him. His only concern was that he'd be disturbed by the lodger. When he remembered the corpse was lying on the floor, he made an effort to dignify it with a blanket before running the taps and chucking a number of items into the sink. Before leaving, he picked up a small mahogany case containing sixty specially-made cigarettes and left. Interested in his bizarre behaviour, and conscious it might be of some relevance further down the line, Bland asked again about the items he put in the sink.

'Yes, I did turn the tap on in the sink in the kitchen at Cheyne Walk where I had left the body. The first thing I threw in was a handbag, then a dishcloth and a towel, some knives, plates, I think a saucer and maybe some shoes. It was mainly things that came to hand. I remember her shoes had come off because I saw her toes protruding through her stockings.'

After leaving Cheyne Walk, Mackay crossed Albert Bridge and made his way to Jack's Place, a Western-style restaurant in Battersea. He ate a meal and then went to visit his friends, the Cowdreys, for a drink. He also revealed that he'd taken the mahogany cigarette box back to the home of Rev Brack, where he destroyed it with a hammer and 'scattered it to the four winds'. Not wishing to waste the contents, he smoked the cigarettes. 'Nobody ever saw that box,' he said. 'I made sure of it.'

Bland asked for more details about how Mackay covered Isabella's body.

'I left her lying on her back on the kitchen floor, arms folded over her body, covered as I told you, her head was close to the oven, the door of which was open,' he said. 'The door was already open, I did not open it. Her legs were facing towards the entrance leading into the kitchen.'

'Did you take any keys away with you?'

'I'm pretty sure I didn't. I am absolutely sure,' he said.

Although he denied it, Mackay must have taken the keys because the house was locked behind him.

* * *

The disclosures made by Mackay did not stop with the murder of Isabella Griffiths. Bland went on to question him about a string of robberies, in chronological order. Mackay even admitted to stealing two handbags from a house in Crowborough, Sussex, miles away from his usual stomping ground. At one point, Bland asked about the knifepoint robbery of Lady Becher on Boxing Day, 1974, where he made off with £115 and a silver medallion.

'Hang on a sec,' said Mackay. 'Becher strikes a bell but I have never had that much cash in one snatch. I have had a good deal but never that much cash in one go. It sounds like my method because I have done jobs with a knife but I honestly cannot remember this one. If I can recollect it I will tell you. As I have said, the name rings a bell and it does sound like my method.'

Bland asked about another Chelsea robbery that took place on 10 February, where the culprit posed as a security officer. Mackay confessed immediately:

'Yes that was definitely me. That is the one I was concerned about, more than all of them because I had had a fair conversation with her and when I went up to the fifth floor with her I put my hand around her neck. I think it was my right hand on this occasion because sometimes I use my right hand, other times my left. I remember squeezing the woman's throat hard. I actually thought I had murdered her because she blacked out and her legs started twitching. Someone came along, a woman saw what was happening around the corner, she caught me red handed, otherwise I think I would have murdered her. I snatched her handbag and bolted. I remember as I ran past the woman who was looking I knocked something out of her hand. It was china or crockery of some sort.'

Then came the crucial admission, the robbery that had nailed Mackay. It was 15 February 1975 and the victim was Margaret Diver.

'This woman was very hospitable under the circumstances,' said Mackay. 'I drank my tea standing up. I did not sit down. There is a strong possibility that I spoke to this woman about Tooting Bec. After the tea I rushed out and picked up her bag, which was lying near a chair by the front door.'

Bland asked about a few more robberies, but then he realized he'd left one out. Mackay's confession to this crime would later prove vital in establishing where he had been on the day of the Ivy Davies murder. 'I have taken this one out of rotation,' said Bland. 'It happened on February 3, 1975, in Red Lion Square.' He showed Mackay a silver pen inscribed with 'L. R. Chairman A.C.W.W. 1947–1953'.

'Yes, I did the one where that pencil was stolen,' said Mackay. 'I cannot remember the exact details.'

As the confessions came tumbling out, he became deflated, as if the futility of his actions were dawning on him. 'This was becoming a disease,' he said. 'It started off in December with one or two every couple of weeks and then it built up until I was doing one every day, or every other day, and in some cases more than one a day.'

As disturbing as they were, solving the spree of violent robberies was much less important than securing confessions to the murders. After all, the immediate danger was off the streets. As Mackay owned up to crime after crime, Bland knew he must be put away for a very long time.

He asked again about 10 March 1975, the day Adele Price was murdered in Lowndes Square. Mackay revealed how he inveigled his way into the widow's flat and played another cruel trick before killing her.

'I wandered around Knightsbridge and then went into Harrods. It's that large store,' he said, as if Bland might mistake the world-famous department store for a corner shop.

He admitted he was cruising 'for a likely pick-up, anybody who might be a fair chance to follow.' Finding no-one there, he moved along to Belgravia where he had something to eat and then sat in a park. He explained:

> 'This was in a small square next to the square where the woman was killed. I sat for a further hour and a quarter drinking a half bottle of scotch. This did not get me drunk. It just stimulated me. I looked across the street and saw the lady involved in the murder cross the street onto my side. I stopped as if lost, awaited to see which building she would enter. When she entered the building I made to fumble with my keys. She had opened the door by this time and I slipped in behind her. She turned around, looked a little startled, I waved my keys and said, "Oops, sorry madam".
>
> 'She then closed the front door and I made my way up the stairs. I stopped at the top of the stairs and had a slight tremor in my leg. She then came up the stairs and she said to me, "Is there something the matter?" I said I felt a little faint. She asked me if there was anything she could do for me. I said that I didn't know but it would perhaps be a help if I could have a cup of tea or a glass of water. She said she would get me a glass of water or perhaps make me a cup of tea and I said, "No thank you, water will do."'

'Could you describe this woman to me?' asked Bland.

> 'I think the woman wore glasses and something on her head. I don't know if it was a scarf type hat or an ordinary hat. She definitely had a hat on of some sort. She wore a sort of thick ordinary

outdoor coat and had a stick. The tremor in my leg, I think was nerves. She told me to wait in the parlour which was just inside her front door. By that I mean it was a type of a hallway immediately inside the front door. She went into a little room, which I thought was the kitchen but later turned out to be her bathroom. When her back was turned I slammed the front flat door and whisked into the room where the TV was and into her kitchen. She came out of the bathroom and I was out of her vision at this time and heard her exclaim, "Oh how odd." She opened her front door and closed it back again. She was mumbling something. I couldn't comprehend what she was saying, she seemed to have the impression that I had departed from the flat. I think this was the general idea at the back of my mind when I slammed the front door and whisked away. By this I meant by getting out of sight quietly and quickly.

'By this time I was of one of two minds, either to ask her for cash or to call it off. She came into the kitchen, stated in shocked surprise that she thought I had gone. I told her that I did not want any complications and that I was feeling on edge. I looked around the room and stated that this was Belgravia, you must know what I'm here for. She said, "I can well guess." I told her to go into the bedroom, she went there. I seemed to go into the bedroom with her.

'The next thing I remember I had my hand around her neck. I don't remember what hand or how I did it or even why I did it. It seemed to happen so much quicker than in the Cheyne Walk one where I seemed to have lots of time. As I was strangling her she seemed to sink down onto the floor. I didn't particularly think about whether she was dead or not. I went into the TV room, switched on the TV and gazed out of the window for quite some time. That is overlooking the square. I don't exactly or roughly know how long I looked out of the window but I got tired of standing at the window. I went over to the front door and put the catch down. I went into the kitchen. I opened the French windows, leaned over and I was there for roughly five or seven minutes leaning on the parapets. Then I went back into the room and noticed a radio on the coffee table. It had a small aerial.

'I went back into the bedroom where the woman was lying on the floor and took another radio. I put them in my pocket, wandered about a bit, sat on the settee. I started to think what I had done with my life. I didn't particularly think about murdering the old woman. It didn't strike me particularly that I was in a serious situation. I don't know what happened after that, I may have dropped off for a while. The next thing I remember I heard a rattling sound and this seemed to wake me up. This rattling was coming from the direction of the front door.

'The TV was still on. I got up and the rattling ceased. I didn't hear anybody shout or say anything from the other side of the door, all I heard was rattling. I undid the chain on the door, I had put this on at the same time as I put the catch on. I opened the door and I didn't see anybody in the passage at all. The buzzer, very strong, went as I opened the door and seemed to decrease as the door closed. I went down the stairs and as I was doing so a girl came up. She was in her late 20s or early 30s. Just before this I seemed to remember one of the doors opening in the flat above and a man put his head out. It shot back in again. I heard his door slam.

'This girl that passed me on the stairs may have been younger than I thought. She spoke to me, she said something about wanting some help because she couldn't get into her flat: "What can I do? I'm locked out?" I said to her, "Then you had better see the porter."

'She said, "I've already spoken to the porter, I'll have to try again." I came down the stairs. As I did so the girl also came out and I saw that she used the intercom at the front door. As I came away from the place I turned right towards Knightsbridge. I remember passing the Park Tower Hotel. I wandered about that area and made my way to the King's Road and I went into an off-licence and bought myself another bottle of whisky. This was a half bottle. I can't remember exactly what off-licence it was but seem to remember it was next to a store that sold very old furniture.'

'What else did you steal at the flat when you murdered the woman?' asked Bland.

'I think I took cash from her handbag, which was in the bedroom,' responded Mackay. 'There was a lot of better things to take from the flat but I don't think I was particularly interested. All I took from there was the cash from the handbag and the two radios.'

Mackay was shown a screwdriver and asked whether he took it from there. He said it was not his. 'It would be too big to use on a lock and I would not carry it as an offensive weapon because I carry two knives,' he said. He was also asked about a nylon stocking found in a drinks cupboard in the hallway.

'If it was there it would appear I must have used it,' he said. 'I may have used it to tie around the woman's neck but I don't think I did. I used my hands. That would be the only reason I would use a nylon stocking.'

This comment was odd, because Mackay had made no admission of ever using a nylon stocking in a crime and neither had he been accused of doing so. Later he would be asked about a murder in which one was used, and another murder in which one may have been used. A third murder would also involve an attempt to remove a woman's stockings. Was he referring to one of those cases when he talked about using a stocking in a crime? If not, then why did he suggest he might use one?

Bland asked whether Mackay drew the curtains in Adele Price's flat after he killed her. He said he did. He also admitted rifling through drawers in the house. After Mackay left the flat, he said he continued to walk the streets 'polishing off' the bottle of scotch he had bought earlier.

'Frankly I do not remember what happened to me the rest of this night,' he told Bland. 'I was so drunk. It is possible one of two things — I either went back to my regular haunt at Stockwell or caught a taxi at Chelsea Bridge to Leicester Square then a tube to East Finchley. But I'm pretty sure the state I was in I must have caught a taxi, because I couldn't see myself walking that distance to Stockwell without sobering up. Of course, it is possible I may have sobered up enough to walk to Stockwell or even get a cab that would accept me. I do remember this night that I walked past Cheyne Walk.'

He added that he sold one of the radios to a 'coloured man' in the Royal Oak pub in Clapham, for £3. The other one he disposed of in the tunnel at Stockwell Road tube station a few days later, on the night he apparently tried to kill himself, leading to him being sectioned in hospital. 'There was a little incident in there of me trying to strangle myself,' he added, helpfully.

Mackay made a number of further admissions to robberies, about twenty-five in total, several of them without prompting.

'Oh, I just remembered another one,' he said on one occasion, as if casting his mind back to a fond memory. Bland then decided to ask about the murder of the homeless man Mackay had voluntarily confessed to. His account was detached and matter of fact. He revealed it had taken place before the Isabella Griffiths murder:

'This was in the early hours, 2.30am I think, sometime in January 1974. It was before I killed the woman in Cheyne Walk. I had been drinking in pubs in the Clapham area and when they closed I walked from Stockwell up to the Embankment and walked along the side of the River Thames. No, I'm sorry, I didn't go straight to the Embankment I went to the Elephant and Castle, then I veered off towards Hungerford Bridge. It took me quite some time to get there because I had bought a half bottle of scotch before the pubs closed and was drinking as I went along. I cannot remember the exact route I took but I went past the Pavilion Buildings which is at the Festival Hall. I crossed over Hungerford Bridge which is going from south to north, as I said earlier it was about 2.30am. The weather was nippy but I wasn't cold.

'Halfway over the bridge I saw a vagrant coming from north to south, which means he was coming towards me. He was late 40s to 50. He wore a sort of cap affair, a shabby grease cap. He had some growth on his face as if he hadn't shaved for some time. He was wearing an overcoat. I think it was whitish or greyish. He was about 5ft 8. He gave me the impression he was of medium build. As he came towards me I could see that he had been drinking himself and he shouted some abuse at me. I can't remember what he said but something like,

"Eff off" or "Fuck off". He was sort of growling. He waved his arms in the air towards me. It was at that time that I lost my temper. I grabbed him by his pants at the backside and his neck, that is the collar at the back of his coat, and heaved him over the edge of the bridge, into the River Thames. Again, this seemed to happen very quickly. I looked over the bridge and the water sprayed up. He must have gone under and then I saw him come up. He started splashing as though he couldn't swim. I can't remember if he shouted but I suppose he did. He was splashing a lot.'

'Can you swim?' asked Bland.

'Yes.'

'Did you think of going in after him?'

'No I didn't. I just lost my temper and just threw him in. I didn't care if he sank or not. I think I stayed that night at Charing Cross Station. The next morning, I went back to my home at Finchley. I was staying with the Reverend Brack at that stage.'

In total, the statement took more than four hours to write. Once it was completed, Mackay was charged with the murders of Isabella Griffiths and Adele Price and two specimen cases of robbery. To each charge Mackay, who was in the presence of his solicitor, said, 'I don't wish to say anything.'

But he did have more to tell.

Chapter 8

A Stranger at the Door

Patrick Mackay was finally going to face justice for the campaign of terror he had brought to the West End, and the unimaginable violence he had inflicted on Father Crean. If it wasn't for the obvious problem that there was no name, or indeed body, to tie Mackay to the death of the homeless man on Hungerford Bridge, John Bland would have charged him with four counts of murder, instead of three. Now, after hearing about his arrest, detectives from other parts of London started examining their own unsolved murder files. They had names and faces to put to victims, but no suspects. Two unsolved crimes in particular seemed to fit Mackay's modus operandi: the murders of Mary Hynes on 20 July 1973, and shopkeeper Frank Goodman on 13 June 1974. Yet when questioned, Mackay was considerably less forthcoming on those matters than he had been about the other killings.

Like many of Mackay's victims, Mary Hynes was an elderly spinster. Her real name was Bridget, although she was also known as Molly. To add to the confusion, the correct spelling of her surname was Hynds. For the purposes of this book, I have continued to use the name Mary Hynes because it has been associated with the Mackay case for more than forty years. Unlike Mackay's other elderly, female victims,

Mary did not reside in one of the fancier parts of London. The 73-year-old lived alone in a three-room, ground-floor flat at 4 Willes Road, Kentish Town, north-west London. The area was a short distance from vibrant Camden Town and has been home to a number of creative people, including the writer George Orwell and Scottish folk singer Bert Jansch.

Mary Hynes was something of a wanderer. Originally from Northern Ireland, where she was raised in a brood of ten, she had moved to London in the hope of a better life. But decades later, that life ended in tragedy when she was found bludgeoned to death with a piece of wood. Adding to the ignominy of her final moments, a stocking was stuffed in her mouth after she died.

Kind-hearted Mary was known for sitting on benches outside Kentish Town Railway Station and elsewhere in the area, where she would chat with homeless people and the elderly. She also drank regularly in the Assembly Rooms pub and the Wolseley Arms in Kentish Town. She was known for being unfailingly nice, polite and having a fondness for animals; she would often stop and pet dogs while chatting to their owners in the street. Mary was a beloved local character who was recognizable from afar due to her slight limp.

Heating engineer Brian Johnson lived with his wife, Rosemary, on the top floor of 4 Willes Road and often did odd jobs for Mary. He had the questionable honour of being a tenant of his mother-in-law, Hannah Carter. She occupied two rooms on the same floor as Mary, who paid her £5 a week in rent. A few weeks before she was found dead, Mary complained that somebody had stolen £5 from her room, but there was no sign of a break-in. Police were never able to establish whether the alleged theft was a relevant factor in her murder. Mary did most of her socializing in the pub or out on the street, so there were few visitors, apart from a nephew from Birmingham and a social worker. Hannah said a sister, called May, would also visit occasionally.

Brian saw Mary at 5.30pm on 19 July when they exchanged pleasantries on the doorstep. Hannah reported hearing the front door slam at about 7pm the next day, shortly after Brian and Rosemary went out. Two days later the rent had not been paid and Brian and his mother-in-law grew concerned for their neighbour. 'We always knew when Miss Hynes was in because she would have her light on even during the day as it's very dark at the back of the house,' Brian later told police. 'My mother-in-law asked me if I would see if Miss Hynes was okay, as she was worried about her as she hadn't left the rent out, which is due on a Saturday morning and Miss Hynes never used to miss. Miss Hynes always used to play her radio on a Saturday morning and when my mother-in-law said she was worried, I remembered I hadn't heard the radio.'

The pair went to investigate. The front door was locked so they went around to the back. Peering through a bedroom window, Brian was horrified to see Mary lying prone on the floor. Her bare legs stuck out from under an eiderdown covering the top part of her body. He told his mother-in-law to call an ambulance. The back door was nailed shut, so he climbed in through an unlocked window and headed to the bedroom, noticing that the key was not in the lock.

'Things were knocked about,' he said. 'I noticed blood up the wall and on the ceiling. I also noticed dried, dark blood on the pillow, which was still on the bed.'

Ambulance officer David Gilhead was next on the scene. He removed the eiderdown and noticed Mary was lying on the floor with her shoulders and hand resting on the bed.

'We could see, looking at the woman, that she had not died of natural causes and death had occurred violently,' he said. 'This was due to the fact that she had a stocking pushed in her mouth and she was badly bruised about the head, face and neck. I then went to put the eiderdown back and went to try the front door, which was locked without any sign of a key.'

Whoever killed Mary Hynes had apparently removed the keys from both the bedroom and the front door.

Gilhead's colleague, Eric Talmadge, also described the scene: 'She was half on her knees facing towards us, with her legs bent under her. She was half propped against the bed. I saw that she had a wound just below the throat and a wound on her forehead. I looked up at the ceiling and noticed there were splashes of blood there.'

Although Hannah told police she had seen Mary walking with a tall, 'sharp-featured' man in his 60s on 15 July, the man was never traced.

On 22 April 1975, Mackay was again interviewed by DSUP John Bland at Canon Row Police Station, along with DCI Gerring and DS Ramsay. The Mary Hynes case had obvious similarities with the murders of Isabella Griffiths and Adele Price. Mary fitted the age profile of Mackay's other victims and it appeared that she had been beaten and strangled, just like Isabella Griffiths and Adele Price. And while the stocking stuffed in her mouth was not a hallmark of Mackay's other crimes, he had spoken of using stockings while being interviewed.

When Bland read the case notes two additional things stood out. Firstly, the front door had been locked by the killer, just as it had been with Isabella Griffiths and Father Crean. Secondly, Mary's body had been partly covered by an eiderdown. Again, this echoed how the bodies had been left at other crime scenes. If Mackay was not responsible for this murder, then an equally cruel and vicious killer was on the loose.

Bland began the interview by cautioning Mackay and reminding him of his rights. He then asked if he'd ever been to Kentish Town.

'I've wandered all over London,' he replied. 'I like riding on the tubes and on the buses.'

'Can you remember being in Kentish Town in July 1973?' asked Bland.

'Yeah, well not really at that time. I know I've been to Kentish Town because it's next to Camden Town.'

Bland told Mackay about the murder of Mary Hynes. Mackay paused.

'Have you photographs of the house?' he asked. Bland promised to show him later. 'You know I remember being in Kentish Town and knocking on a door asking for water,' he volunteered. 'I remember the house because it had some trees or a big hedge at the side of it. I remember an old lady answering the door and giving me a glass of water. Could this be the same house?'

'Until we get the photographs and you recognize the house or otherwise I can't say.'

'How did she die?' asked Mackay.

At that point Bland paused the interview. Whether this was a tactic to let Mackay stew on the idea nobody knows. The transcript says the pair spent the next ten minutes smoking and 'talking generally' while waiting for fresh coffee before resuming the interview. Whatever happened during that time, it certainly jogged Mackay's memory.

'She was murdered by being hit over the head with a piece of wood,' explained Bland. 'After being murdered, a stocking was stuffed into her mouth and I think one was tied around her throat. Her body was covered with an eiderdown. I must be fair Patrick, this appears identical to the method you used because not only was the body covered, as in the Cheyne Walk job, but the doors were locked and the keys were taken away which, as you must admit, is your method.'

'Yes, I must admit that it appears similar, but I just can't remember,' said Mackay. 'I know I went to a door for water and that was in Kentish Town and I know something about stockings, but I just can't remember.'

Bland could go no further with Mackay because the Mary Hynes case was not under his jurisdiction. That honour fell to DCI John Harris, who was based at Albany Street

Police Station. He'd been investigating the Mary Hynes case from the outset and, until Mackay's arrest, had been as stumped as the West End robbery squad. He arrived at the station with ten photographs from the scene, for Mackay's benefit, not his own. Harris had witnessed the gruesome aftermath of the murder with his own eyes and was present at the post-mortem, and when Mary's body was identified by her distraught sister. Harris felt a personal desire to bring Mary's killer to justice, and he was about to come face to face with the man he believed was responsible.

'If you can help clear my mind, I will tell you what I know,' Mackay told him. He reiterated that he remembered going to a house in Kentish Town and asking for a glass of water, and said he knew something about a stocking, but couldn't recall the details. 'I would like to clear it all up,' he offered helpfully.

Mackay was shown a photograph of the exterior of 4 Willes Road. 'That looks like the house I went to but I got the impression it was at the end of a road,' he said. In fact, the house appeared to be the last in the street because the actual last house was set back and obscured by bushes. Mackay was shown a photo of the back of the property and remarked, 'that doesn't ring a bell at all.' He was then shown three photos of the inside of the house, including one of Mary's body. 'No that means nothing to me,' he said.

'The method used to kill this old lady was very similar to the method you used in Chelsea,' said DCI Harris, referring to the murder of Isabella Griffith. 'Not only was she hit a number of times over the head but the body was covered and the door of the flat was locked, and the keys were taken away. What do you say about that?'

'It certainly sounds like me and I would help you if I could only remember, but I just can't remember anything.'

'You know Kentish Town I believe?'

'Yes, I know Kentish Town. I used to go there a lot, or at least to Camden Town a lot, and I went through Kentish

Town to get there. I used to get a bus to the West End where they turned around under the bridge.'

'You mean Camden Street?'

'I don't know the name of it.'

'Do you really mean to tell me you remember so much about Camden Town but cannot remember whether you killed this old lady? It was shortly after you went to live at Finchley.' Harris was more aggressive in his questioning than officers Brown and Hart. Perhaps Mackay closed down because he viewed him as an enemy, someone who didn't deserve his help.

'I really can't remember,' he replied. 'I have told you I would help you if I can but so many things are a blank.'

With that, Mackay's first full interview in connection with the Mary Hynes case came to an end. But DCI Harris tried again, nearly three weeks later, on 3 July. This time, Mackay was brought to the detective's office in Albany Street and interviewed in the presence of Acting Detective Inspector Mansbridge and Mackay's solicitor, Robin Clark. Harris started by warning Mackay that he did not want him to confess if he was not guilty.

'No, of course not. I wouldn't do that, but I want to help as much as possible and clear up the things I have done,' replied Mackay. But his memory was still hazy. He recalled details of the outside of Mary Hynes' home and the tops of the windows. Although he had seen photographs of the house, the detectives felt his ability to recall its appearance was the result of personal experience and strongly suggested his guilt.

'Can you tell me what happened when you went to the house and how you got the glass of water?' pressed Harris.

'I knocked at the door. An old lady came to the door and I asked for a glass of water. She shuffled away down the passage and came back later with the water.'

'When you say she shuffled, what exactly do you mean?'

'Well she shuffled. She seemed to hobble along as though she had rheumatism in her leg. I do remember she was wearing slippers.' Harris nodded. It was true that Mary walked with a limp.

'Can you describe the woman more fully?'

'Well she was old, I should think in her late 60s maybe 70s. She was certainly old. She had greyish black hair, not very tidy, but then I wouldn't say she was scruffy.'

'Can you remember what she was wearing?'

'No, I can't. Except I do remember she was wearing slippers.'

'I think you have mentioned something about stockings in connection with a woman in Kentish Town. Could you tell me about that?'

'It's a bit hazy,' said Mackay. 'I do remember I stuffed stockings into an old lady's mouth.'

'Was it this woman that gave you the glass of water?'

'I can't remember if it was the same woman but I do remember asking for a glass of water and I do remember stuffing stockings down an old lady's throat. If this was the only old lady that had stockings stuffed in her throat, then it must have been me that did it but I just can't remember whether it was the same woman.'

'I don't want to know what you think happened or what you now surmise happened, I want to know what you can remember about actual occurrences,' said Harris. 'We'll try and help you to remember these as we go on.'

'Fair enough. Thank you very much.'

'We'll leave these stockings for a moment, we'll just go through this gradually and see what you can remember. Now when this woman went to collect the glass of water, where did she go? Did she turn off to the left or right or go straight down the passage and through a door? Did you see where she got the water from?'

'I must try and remember this...Yes, I remember. She walked down the passage, she turned right at the end and I lost sight of her. She then came back from that direction with a glass of water.'

'Are you sure she turned right at the end of the passage?'

'Yes, I'm sure. Now I think about it, I am sure.'

'What happened when she came back?'

'I remember getting hold of this woman and I remember pushing her down the passage.'

'How did you push her down the passage?'

'I remember holding her from behind by her elbows and pushing and steering her down the passage.' Mackay's description of his behaviour was similar to the way he had treated robbery victims Margaret Diver and Ilma Lewis.

'What happened to make you do this?'

'I remember that when she came back with the water I was angry that she had opened the door to a stranger and I told her that she shouldn't open the door to strangers. I just seemed to go mad then and I got hold of her by the elbows and pushed her down the passageway.'

'What happened next?'

'I can't remember. I just can't remember what happened, it's all very hazy. I still get this picture of an old lady with a stocking stuffed in her throat.'

'Are we talking about this same old lady that gave you the water?'

'I just don't know. I keep getting that picture.'

'Well, we'll leave that for a moment and take it step by step and see if you can remember. Now when you got to the end of the passage what happened? Which way did you turn?'

'We turned right, as I mentioned earlier and I seem to remember we turned left into a bedroom.'

'That is possible. What happened next?'

'I can't remember what happened in the flat, the only thing I can remember is stuffing stockings into this lady's mouth. I remember her laying on the floor with the stockings stuffed in her mouth.'

'Now you've never mentioned she was laying on the floor before. Are we now talking about the same woman?'

'Yes, I think it must be. I remember her lying on the floor.'

'Which way was she facing?'

'I can't remember that at all.'

'Now just think about this woman lying on the floor. If you cast your mind back, what can you remember about it?'

'I can remember the face looking up with stockings stuffed in the mouth and I remember marks on the face.'

'What sort of marks were they?'

'I don't know, I just remember marks. I think they may have been cuts.'

'Can you remember whether you caused these marks?'

'No, I don't remember doing anything, but I do remember stuffing the stockings into her mouth. I do remember when she was lying on the floor she had a big hole underneath her chin.'

At this point, Mackay used his thumb to indicate where the wound had been. Harris asked whether the woman already had the wound when she brought the glass of water to the door.

'No of course she didn't,' he replied irritably. Harris felt Mackay was holding back. Perhaps the presence of his solicitor was having an effect, encouraging him not to give too much away.

'Then are we now saying this is the same woman, with the stockings stuffed in her mouth and the wound under the chin, that brought you the water?'

'Yes, I can now remember. It was the same woman but I don't remember what else I did in the flat.'

'Can you remember exactly what position this woman was in when she was laying on the floor?'

'She was lying on her back with her arms to her sides. I remember now she had bare arms, I don't know why I remember that but I do. She definitely had bare arms.'

'If you picture this woman lying on the floor, can you remember if there is anything near the head?'

'No, I can't remember that at all.'

'Can you remember whether you moved the woman after you saw her on the floor?'

'What do you mean?'

'Well did you try and pick her up and put her on the bed?'

'I may have done. I would do that out of a sense of decency, but I can't remember doing it.'

'Do you remember whether you covered the body with an eiderdown?'

'No, I can't remember that either but again it's the sort of thing I would do, out of a sense of decency.'

'If you can remember about the body lying on the floor and about stuffing the stockings into her mouth, can you remember hitting her with anything?'

'I can remember pushing her along the passage. I can remember stuffing the stockings into her throat and I remember her lying on the floor. I may have tied a stocking round her mouth, I just can't remember that. But I don't remember hitting her with anything.'

'Can you remember anything else about the flat?'

'No, I can't remember anything else at all.'

Mackay paused. 'There is one thing I remember about the flat and that is the back door.'

'What about the back door?'

'I seem to remember it was black and it was nailed up. I couldn't open it and I saw that it was nailed up.'

'This is significant,' said Harris. Mackay was correct, the back door had been nailed shut. 'Can you remember anything else about the back door?'

'No, I don't even remember where the back door was in the flat, but I do remember clearly there was a back door, which I tried to open but it had nails in and I couldn't move it.'

'I have in the past, and this morning, showed you some photographs,' said DCI Harris. 'Have I ever shown you a photograph with the back door in it?'

'No, I don't think so.'

'Now you agree that the woman did not have any wounds under her chin or marks on her face when she opened the door to you in the first place or when she brought you the water?'

'That's right.'

'Was anybody else with you?'

'No.'

'So, if this woman had wounds under her chin and other injuries to her head you must have caused them?'

'Yes, I must have done but I don't remember doing it.'

Mackay had coughed to the murder of Mary Hynes. Or so police believed. DCI Harris showed him a photograph of Mary lying on the floor with a wound under her chin. Mackay said the wound appeared as he remembered it. Certain that Mackay had killed Mary Hynes, Harris arranged for him to be driven to 4 Willes Road to view the property. Peering out from the back of a police van Mackay remarked, 'I'm sure that is the house I called at.' He was driven past again and added, 'Yes I can positively say that is the house I went into, there is no doubt of that at all.' He was then taken back to the station where he had a meal. At 2.40pm, Mackay was brought back to the office, with his solicitor, where DCI Harris told him, under caution, he was 'quite satisfied' Mackay had killed Mary Hynes. Before taking the decision to charge him, Harris asked about the missing door keys.

'What I normally do is lock the door and take the keys with me,' said Mackay. 'I've got a thing about keys. I don't normally keep them, I usually throw them away. I don't remember doing it on this occasion though.'

'It is quite feasible that's what you would have done?' asked Harris.

'Oh yes, I probably would have done it but I don't remember doing it.'

'Can you now remember why all this took place?' asked Harris.

'I do remember saying, "You shouldn't open the door to strangers,"' he replied. 'I stepped into the hallway and grabbed hold. She turned and I grabbed her elbows and pushed her straight into the bedroom.'

'Was she making a noise and shouting?'

'She wasn't yelling. She seemed in a state of shock.'

'From what you have told me I am quite satisfied that you killed this woman.'

Mackay agreed. 'It's too much to suppose that anyone else killed her, so I must have,' he said. 'But I can't remember the actual killing.'

'Would you like to make a written statement under caution?' asked DCI Harris.

'Yes, I would.'

'Would you like to write that statement yourself?'

'No, you can write for me.'

Mackay dictated a statement to Mansbridge and signed it. It included the following: 'Although I cannot remember the details I am sure that I, and only I, could have committed this murder. I am positive of that. I would like to say that when I knocked on her door the only thought in my mind was to get a glass of water. It was when I told her that she shouldn't answer the door to strangers and having said it to her I just flipped and lost my head.'

DCI Harris officially charged him with his fourth count of murder and Mackay virtually thanked him for doing so. 'As I have said, it's too much to suppose that anybody else killed her,' he added. 'This is a great weight off my mind now. I have been worrying about this.'

It was not exactly what American cops call a 'slam-dunk' confession. Mackay appeared to remember important details about the house, including the fact the back door was nailed shut. He also remembered the way Mary Hynes 'shuffled' as a result of her limp. Added to that, he insisted he had pushed his way into the flat and could remember stuffing a stocking

149

down Mary's throat. There was also the sensible point — made by Mackay himself — that it was 'too much to suppose' that somebody else was going around brutally murdering old ladies, making bizarre efforts to cover their corpses and then leaving locked doors behind them.

But there was a significant sticking point. DCI Harris had seen Mackay's custody records, which said he was locked up at Ashford Remand Centre on the day of the murder, after being arrested for trying to attack a homeless man with a metal pole five days earlier on 15 July 1973. How could the detective make the charge stick?

Efforts were made to investigate conditions at the remand centre and Harris decided it was feasible that Mackay absconded and returned after killing Mary Hynes. He included this in his report:

'I have made enquiries to establish that the Mackay charged with the murder is in fact the same Mackay who was on remand in Ashford. It is of interest that the governor of Ashford at that time suffered a nervous breakdown at about the period in which Mackay was there or shortly afterwards. The officers at that prison, also at the same time, were taking various forms of industrial action and striking because of dissatisfaction over pay. In spite of this, however, there is nothing to show that Mackay either legally or illegally left prison. The security at Ashford is such that I feel it would be impossible for any person to climb the outer fence. It is difficult to see how, if he had left the prison, he would enter again [except] by leaving and re-entering in civilian clothes via the main gate, which I consider possible at that time.'

In a letter to the Director of Public Prosecutions, dated 26 August 1975, Mackay's solicitors officially withdrew his confession. They said that if there was a trial he would deny being present at 4 Willes Road and murdering Mary Hynes. Intriguingly, the letter said that 'due to the passage of time he cannot remember his precise movements on those days.' The suggestion was that Mackay would deny being present at Willes Road, but not necessarily because he had an alibi to prove he was still in custody.

Is it possible that Mackay absconded from the remand centre? He had a history of walking out of special schools and psychiatric institutions dating back to his teens. He hated being incarcerated and he would certainly have taken the first opportunity to walk out of Ashford if it had presented itself. He was also only being held on remand, so he would have had access to his civilian clothes. But having escaped, would he have walked back into custody of his own accord? It seems unlikely as Mackay despised being locked up. However, he had presented himself to doctors before, albeit not for any meaningful periods of time. And he may also have had the clarity of mind to realize that being in detention could be his best chance of establishing an alibi for the murder he had just committed. Although Mackay claimed to forget many details about events, he was no fool, and was capable of acts of cunning when it suited him. He was also experienced at planning robberies and staking out victims before striking, so it stands to reason he would have been equally capable of thinking about how to get away with a murder when an exceptional opportunity presented itself.

When the case appeared at the Old Bailey the charge was allowed to lie on file. By that time, the police had stopped investigating the murder of Mary Hynes and would never re-open the case. The confession would never be tested in front of a jury, and neither Mackay nor the remand centre governor had to face questions about his whereabouts on that day. In his prison memoir Mackay said he went to view the house in Willes Road and suggested he was being flippant when he made the confession. 'She was found stabbed I believe, and battered to death,' he wrote. 'There is no evidence to tie me, except statements I made in a fed-up and couldn't-care-less frame of mind.'

* * *

It is important to remember that Patrick Mackay was not the only man committing murders in London between 1973 and 1975. For every crime committed by Mackay, detectives were dealing with dozens of other serious incidents, including murders. As a result, officers were keen to solve serious crimes as quickly as possible. Sometimes, that involved corrupt practices such as planting evidence or writing up so-called 'verbals'. But often, when a suspect could not be found in a short space of time, detectives would find new events overtaking their investigation and resources became stretched. In difficult cases — such as that of Frank Goodman — it could lead them to remaining unsolved for decades.

Frank, also known as Leslie, was killed in his sweet shop in Rock Street, Finsbury Park, in North London, on or around 13 June 1974. It was about four months after Mackay killed his 'first' confirmed victim, Isabella Griffiths in Chelsea. At the time, the psychopath was living relatively nearby, on Cedar Lawn Avenue in Barnet. The distance between Barnet and Finsbury Park was an eight-mile walk, which would have taken Mackay nearly three hours, but it was just a few stops on the tube and the shop was a thirty second walk from Finsbury Park Station.

Frank was a huge football fan but England had failed to qualify for the imminent 1974 World Cup in West Germany. The national team's failure didn't stop Frank planning to go to a friend's house to watch Brazil take on Yugoslavia in the first game of the tournament on the Thursday afternoon. However, Frank never showed up and on the Monday his body was discovered lying behind the counter in his shop. Frank was probably dead by the time the game kicked off at 5pm.

He had been savagely beaten with a length of gas pipe, his head practically obliterated by repeated blows. A visibly shocked DCSUP Frank McGuiness told reporters at the scene: 'This is the most brutal murder I have ever seen.'

Police issued a timeline that placed the date of death between 13 and 15 June, probably as Frank prepared to close the shop at his customary time of 8.30pm. He was killed with fourteen blows to the head and had tried in vain to defend himself. The assault most likely continued while Frank was unconscious, or even dead. The killer then moved the body to a spot behind the till so he could not be seen through the window, and covered his victim's feet with the shopkeeper's white overcoat. McGuiness was sure that the motive was robbery because bank notes were missing from the till, although bags of change were left behind.

All police had to go on was a bloody footprint found in the shop and the metal pipe, which was recovered nearby. They made a public appeal for bingo players from Finsbury Park's Top Rank club to come forward because they hoped some of its 3,000 members had gone in to buy sweets before going in to play. One widow contacted the local paper, the *Islington Gazette*, to say she had gone into the shop to buy toffees and encountered a tall, black man. She told the paper he was acting suspiciously and Frank was 'quiet and behaving nervously'. She said, 'I thought to myself at the time, "doesn't he seem frightened?" When he spoke to me he had to kind of lean forward towards me.'

Police took a statement from the woman but it was a dead end. But there was one other clue — if only detectives had known where to look. The killer had locked the door behind him, a hallmark of Patrick Mackay's modus operandi. 'The man would have been covered in blood and would have left in daylight,' McGuiness told reporters. 'I feel that someone would have seen him locking up Mr Goodman's shop, as he must have spent some time over it.'

North London detectives were already stretched at the time. Two weeks earlier, a 22-year-old prostitute, Eileen Cotter, was found beaten and strangled in a 'lover's lane' in Hamilton Park, Highbury. Eileen was described as a 'popular girl with a kind heart' and was known for buying soup and hotdogs for vagrants in the Finsbury Park area. In fact, she liked to set out her own stall, so to speak, next to the hot dog stand outside Finsbury Park. Eileen was picked up by a man in a car at 11.45pm but was never seen alive again. McGuiness was placed in charge of both investigations. More than a month after the murder of Frank Goodman, both were still unsolved. It was clear that police were hunting two separate killers, but the *Islington Gazette* could not help but draw parallels between the cases.

'During the last two months this respectable suburb of throbbing London has been ripped apart by murder, gruesome violence and sex,' it wrote. The paper called the murder of Frank Goodman 'the most savage and callous that detectives had seen'. It added: 'The laboratory reports said that he had died from multiple injuries to the head. That was a nice way of putting it. Mr Goodman's head had been smashed out of recognition by a maniac using a piece of gas piping. Not just hit once, but time and time again. Savage, repeated blows. And after the murderer had completed his task he coolly dragged the body round the back of the counter, took the keys and left – locking the door behind him.'

Was the reporter describing the actions of Patrick Mackay? At first glance, Frank Goodman didn't match his usual victim profile. He was not outwardly wealthy — like Adele Price or Isabella Griffiths — although he clearly would have had cash in the shop. He was also not killed in his home after being followed from the street. This meant the murderer didn't have the security of a front door to hide behind when there was the very real risk that someone could walk in. Mackay enjoyed killing in private where he could savour the time spent with the dead bodies. There was also the fact that Mackay didn't know Frank Goodman, or at least there was no evidence to say the pair knew each other. Mackay had been very familiar with at least two of his victims, Isabella Griffiths and Father Anthony Crean. Finsbury Park was also way outside Mackay's usual stalking grounds of Kensington and Chelsea, and it was miles away from the other areas he used to visit, such as Catford where his aunts lived, and Stockwell where he often crashed with the Cowdreys.

But Mackay's commuting habits meant almost anywhere in London was a potential crime scene. The shop was just metres from Finsbury Park tube, where Mackay could make a quick getaway. And although killing someone in what was essentially a public place presented risks that Mackay was not accustomed to taking, he was not particularly shy about committing violent crimes in public. There was the boy he had tried to kill as a youth and, more recently, the tramp he claimed to have thrown off Hungerford Bridge. His unpredictability meant Mackay was theoretically capable of killing anyone, anytime, anyplace.

Another thing to consider is that by the time of Frank Goodman's death, Mackay had only committed two murders (or at least two murders to which he admitted). He killed the homeless man in January 1974 and Isabella Griffiths about a month later. There was no real pattern to Mackay's behaviour at this point, and the robbery campaign against elderly women had not begun in earnest. He was haphazard and didn't necessarily always have a victim type in mind.

The strongest indication of his guilt, as far as detectives were concerned, were the chilling similarities between the murder of Frank Goodman and the killing of Father Crean. The attack on Frank Goodman had been unusually violent. His head was pulverized by repeated blows with a heavy object. Father Crean's skull had been shattered with an axe, after Mackay stabbed him in the head with a knife until the blade snapped. While many people are capable of murder, only a handful of killers are overtaken by the urge to use such frenzied, uncontrolled violence.

Not only were the injuries strikingly similar, but in each case the killer had spent time interacting with the body. In the case of Father Crean, Mackay decided to dignify his corpse by draping a towel over his head. He then wandered around the priest's house, returning periodically to his body to sit and stare. Inside the Rock Street shop, the killer dragged his victim's body behind the counter and draped a coat over his legs. This may have been to disguise the corpse from passers-by, but it may also have served another twisted purpose. Was it done out of a sense of 'decency', as Mackay might put it? Detectives believed the killer had spent some time in the shop. If Mackay was responsible, was this so he could spend time staring at the wounds he had inflicted?

There was also the matter of the locked door. Mackay took the keys with him at numerous robberies, and the murders of Isabella Griffiths and Father Crean. At the time, police believed he had done the same after killing Mary Hynes. Mackay would probably have lingered for longer after killing Adele Price had he not been disturbed. Another indication that made detectives believe Mackay could have killed Frank Goodman was the careless way in which the killer disposed of the murder weapon within feet of the dead body. Furthermore, very little was stolen. Mackay rarely took items of value, particularly after a murder, because the killing was an end in itself.

The transcripts of Mackay's police interviews in relation to the Frank Goodman case are still under lock and key at the National Archives in Kew. I tried to obtain them using Freedom of Information requests, but these were turned down because of concerns about harm to the 'physical or mental' wellbeing of the relatives of the victim and the defendant, despite Frank Goodman having few, if any, living relatives.

As a result, exactly what Mackay said in interview will remain secret for another forty years.

However, Tim Clark and John Penycate, authors of the 1976 book *Psychopath: The Case of Patrick Mackay* did have a chance to read the transcripts in 1975. They recounted how Mackay was quizzed in Brixton Prison and eventually confessed to carrying out a robbery at the shop, because he remembered throwing away his bloodstained boots in Finchley Cemetery. When police took him there in May 1975, he located them easily. Human blood was found on the boots but it could not be identified. The authors said the Cowdreys made statements describing how Mackay turned up at their house that night with cash and cigarettes, while his new landlords in Barnet were able to identify the lead pipe as being taken from their home.

Detectives clearly felt their case was strong enough to bring charges, but as the court date at the Old Bailey approached, Mackay's lawyers made it clear he would plead not guilty. The case was ultimately allowed to lie on file. Exactly why prosecutors didn't take either the Mary Hynes or Frank Goodman case to trial is unclear. Perhaps it was to save time and resources, given that Mackay had already admitted three killings (later to result in convictions for manslaughter by way of diminished responsibility). But perhaps there is another explanation.

Following Mackay's conviction and the revelations about his frequent contact with psychiatric hospitals, the newspapers made a huge issue of the missed opportunities to stop his killing spree. The prospect of the Mary Hynes case going to trial would have concerned not just the governor and staff at Ashford Remand Centre, where Mackay should have been locked up at the time of the murder, but also those higher up the chain, including government ministers. The entire fiasco had the potential to cause huge embarrassment to police and medical professionals, as well as the politicians who might have to take responsibility for a system that had failed to deal with a psychopathic maniac. Three killings to Mackay's name was bad enough. But five? That would have made him equal to London's most infamous serial killer, Jack the Ripper, and a trial would ensure that his case would stay on the front pages for weeks.

With indications from his lawyers that he would admit three counts of manslaughter, and with few close friends or family members to fight for justice for either Mary Hynes or Frank Goodman, it was easier to accept Mackay's not guilty pleas than go to trial. The judge ruled that while there might be enough evidence to bring a case, a trial was not in the public interest, given the other serious charges Mackay had admitted.

As a result, we must accept Mackay's innocence. It is only fair, in that case, to repeat what he wrote in his prison memoir, regarding the Goodman case: 'The truth of the strange case may, in thirty years or so, unfold. Only then will you have your man. This, by the way, will not be me. I am not responsible. But you will be surprised — very much so — when you find out, as they say in detective stories, who done it.'

More than forty years later, the mystery has still not been solved. And neither has that of the murder of Eileen Cotter. But then Mackay was never linked to the Cotter murder. He was, however, linked to five more killings, each as brutal as the ones for which he was convicted.

Chapter 9

Unsolved

Whatever was behind the decision not to take the Mary Hynes and Frank Goodman cases to trial, there were further difficult choices to make behind the scenes. As murder squads across London checked their unsolved files in the hope Mackay might fit the bill as a suspect, it started to look as though he'd go down as one of Britain's worst serial killers. Yet, for a variety of reasons, charges were never brought in five more murders over which he was questioned.

Today, the tragic cases of Heidi Mnilk, Stephanie Britton and Christopher Martin, Sarah Rodmell, and Ivy Davies remain unsolved. As unsolved crimes, the interview transcripts and witness statements will probably never be made public, so exactly what Mackay was asked and how he replied is shrouded in mystery. Yet the details of his other crimes, and what we know about his lifestyle, does allow some insight into whether or not he could have killed these people.

This is not an attempt to apportion blame to Mackay or anyone else, it is simply a review of the publicly available information about the crimes in an attempt to understand why he came under suspicion. Perhaps it could also encourage a witness, or a new suspect, to come forward. Although the unsolved murder cases are reviewed periodically, it is unlikely that they will be actively re-investigated unless new information is received.

Train Ride to Death — The murder of Heidi Mnilk

Shortly after Mackay was arrested for the ferocious killing of Father Anthony Crean, detectives wondered whether his spree had actually started nearly two years earlier, on 8 July 1973, with the slaying of a young German nanny on a train.

One year before the murder, Mackay had been released from his second stint in Moss Side Hospital in Liverpool. Reflecting on his time there, many years later, Mackay said he had 'only the best intentions in the living of my life [but] one cannot, unfortunately, always foresee the certain type of stigmas that can form and come to be for some people in such an imperfect world as this.' It was a typically self-serving comment and can be paraphrased thus: 'I tried, but I couldn't help myself.'

The urge to take a human life had been fermenting inside Mackay for quite some time, and like beer in a barrel his rage was liable to explode without proper handling. He killed his pet tortoise as a child, as well as birds and other small animals. He had also tried to strangle a boy in the street, smashed another's head into the pavement, choked his aunt and frequently attacked his mother and sister. His detention at Moss Side was supposed to cure all that, but for two years he had shared his twisted thoughts with murderers and other deviants, which drove his mania deeper into his psyche. When Mackay returned to his mother's home in Gravesend he settled back into his violent routines immediately.

By the beginning of 1973 he was unemployed, drinking heavily and roaming weekly, if not daily, between London and Kent. This was the time when Mackay's interest in Nazism and fascism really took off and became an obsession. It was also during this period that Mackay's criminal life began in earnest. He started committing burglaries, mostly to steal food. There was also the episode where he tried to strangle the family dog. Then, he stole the cheque from Father Crean and endured the bitter break-up of that relationship. To make matters worse, his mother threw him out and he went to live with Reverend Ted Brack. Things seemed to be coming to a head. According to the official timeline, Mackay stifled his murderous impulses for another six months, before drowning the tramp at Hungerford Bridge in January 1974. But did he really keep himself under control for that long?

On 9 July 1973, Londoners woke to headlines about a particularly callous and brutal murder. The *Daily Express* dubbed it the 'Mystery of Girl on the Line' and subtitled the shocking tale 'Train Ride to Death'. The body of a young woman had been found beside the track on a bridge at Abbey Street, Bermondsey, 400 yards from London Bridge Station. Her handbag was found beside her, with a ticket to West Wickham in Kent still inside.

The girl's identity was later revealed as 18-year-old German nanny Heidi Mnilk. She had been in London, sightseeing, for six days with her 17-year-old friend Doris Thurau. The young women boarded the 4.57pm train from Charing Cross to Hayes in Kent but decided to separate on the train because Heidi preferred to sit in a non-smoking compartment. Doris wanted a cigarette, so the pair split up just before the train pulled out to take them to West Wickham, where they were staying.

Moments after it pulled away Heidi was stabbed in the neck and thrown from the train, which was by now moving at 45mph. Two schoolboys, Andrew Lee and Steven Arnold, were travelling in the next compartment and described Heidi's body as looking like a 'bag of bricks' being hurled onto the tracks.

'After the screams Steve saw something fall from the window,' said Andrew. 'The next thing, I saw a girl lying on the track.' When the train stopped at the next station, the shaken pair saw a man get out from the next carriage and make off. 'He was so close we could have grabbed him but there was a hold up when someone got into our compartment,' continued Andrew. 'I told a porter there was a body on the line. He told his superior but I got the impression that I wasn't believed. The killer looked straight into our compartment and looked straight at Steve. He must have known we saw him. I said to one of the station staff, "Did you see that man?" But by that time he had disappeared.'

In a world before CCTV, the killer vanished into the crowd. He may even have turned round and walked back into the station to continue his journey. Station porter Uriah Johnson was unapologetic about ignoring the boys. 'We thought they were just messing about,' he said. 'One can only blame it on the yobs who cry wolf. It happened once too often.'

Another porter, 19-year-old Williams Harris, said, 'I was busy seeing the train out and the boys were telling me something but I didn't understand at first. I didn't see a man get off the train. Some people got off —three couples I believe. My job means a lot to me and I do the best I can. The first priority is seeing the train safely in and out. I do not get a lot of time to notice people.'

The mistake meant the only witnesses to the incident were the two boys. Fortunately, they were able to give a full description of the suspect, and police issued a photofit. The knifeman was described as aged between 37 and 45, about 5ft 6ins tall with short, brown hair and a tanned or red, spotty complexion. The boys added that the man had a slightly pointed chin, thin lips and was clean shaven. There was one more thing — the man was squinting, as if he had trouble seeing.

Police said thirty other people were travelling on the train at the time. Officers recovered a five-inch bowie knife that the killer had thrown onto the tracks after stabbing Heidi. They examined her gold neck chain and her battered camera containing thirty-six snapshots taken at London landmarks. Detectives believed her killer had followed the girls onto the train and they hoped her photos might hold a clue, but they didn't. DCSUP Bob Ramsey headed up the investigation and said the public response was 'tremendous'. Yet it yielded few results.

The police carried out a reconstruction of the murder, using a policewoman dressed like Heidi, and the boys and police officers travelling in the next carriage. It was broadcast on the evening news. On 11 August, a 20-year-old Covent Garden porter was arrested. He jumped from a police car while being taken to the station. He was questioned but never charged. 'We will find the killer no matter how long the inquiry lasts,' promised Ramsey.

In September another witness came forward with an intriguing clue. A Danish woman, who had been travelling on the line back in March 1973 — four months before the murder — told how she might have met the killer during a frightening encounter in which she felt lucky to have escaped unharmed. She said a young man got on at New Cross and sat next to her. According to the woman, he pulled out a knife and asked, 'Are you German?' The woman replied, 'No, do I look like one?' The man said, 'Yes. I hate Germans, especially German women.'

Police said her description of the knife matched the one used to kill Heidi. Later, when an inquest at Southwark Crown Court delivered a verdict of murder, the coroner said there was a remarkable likeness between the photofit produced after the Danish woman came forward and the one put together from the boys' description of Heidi's attacker.

Was there ever any question of Patrick Mackay committing this crime? Police heard he was bragging about murdering Heidi to other prisoners in Brixton Prison while on remand for killing Father Crean. The two witnesses, Andrew and Steven, came to the prison for an ID parade, as did the Danish woman. But none picked out Mackay. 'It is interesting that three witnesses attended this parade,' Mackay wrote later. 'They were unable to pick anyone out.' That seemed to be the end of the investigation, at least as far as he was concerned.

Later incidents suggested detectives may have been wise to rule him out. In August 1975, when Mackay was already in prison, a young woman called Wendy Hall was attacked by a knife-wielding maniac on a train at Tulse Hill, South London, after boarding at Holborn Viaduct. She was stabbed four times and her attacker left the train at Tooting. Fortunately, Wendy survived. Then in January 1977, 24-year-old Kim Taylor was stabbed three times on a train from Norwood to London Bridge. The attacker fled at Bermondsey. Again, the victim survived.

At the time, police publicly said they believed the same man was responsible for the murder of Heidi Mnilk and may have carried out up to nine attacks on trains over several years, although none had proved fatal. He was never identified.

Detectives can hardly be blamed for putting Mackay in the frame. Apart from his alleged confessions in prison, there was considerable circumstantial evidence against him. At the time of the murder Mackay was living with his aunts in Montacute Road, Catford, a few stops down the line from the scene. The train was heading to Hayes, which is technically in Bromley, south-east London, but originally part of the county where Mackay's mother lived. He may have used the route to visit his family, even though it was not the most direct.

According to the authors of *Psychopath,* Tom Herbert, an ex-docker who shared a house with Mackay's aunts, later claimed to have recognized Mackay from the photofit but decided not to contact the police. However, it has to be acknowledged that the photofit does not particularly resemble Mackay and the description given by the two boys does not match his youthful, albeit alcohol-weathered features. And, of course, they did not pick him out at the ID parade.

But the suspected killer's references to Germany and the comments he made to the Danish woman about having a hatred of women were certainly unusual. Mackay was obsessed with the Nazis, which might theoretically have made him sympathetic to Germans. He was also deeply confused and obviously disturbed. He railed against black people although he was mixed race. It would not be surprising if Mackay expressed his obsession with the Nazis as both admiration and dislike for German people at different times, particularly as his father had been a victim of the Germans during the war. There is certainly no doubt Mackay had a hatred of women, as evidenced by his violence towards his sisters, his mother and the majority of his victims.

There was also the fact that the killer of Heidi Mnilk disposed of the murder weapon by throwing it in the nearest possible place, in this case out of the train door along with his victim's body. Mackay took little care in getting rid of the tools of his murderous trade, and left weapons and other implements behind after killing Isabella Griffiths, Adele Price and Father Crean. The unidentified perpetrator of the later train knife attacks retained his weapon. And that serial knife maniac was clearly more inefficient than Heidi Mnilk's murderer, because his attacks didn't claim any more lives.

One obvious argument against Mackay's involvement is the choice of both victim and location. Most of his victims were elderly women who were robbed or killed in their own homes. Mackay enjoyed having the security of a locked door because he could spend time with his victims after they died, reflecting on their appearance and prowling round their homes. He also made efforts to dignify their corpses and was not in the habit of disposing of bodies in public.

Yet as a child, Mackay had been prone to bouts of violence with boys and girls of all ages. Might he have spied a vulnerable woman — close to his sister's age— and taken a spur-of-the-moment decision to act out a long-held fantasy? Was it really so out of character for him to suddenly attack a stranger? He had almost strangled a boy in the street; he did not particularly care when neighbours saw him torturing animals and he was far from shy about attacking his own family members. He admitted killing the tramp on Hungerford Bridge and dumping him in the Thames simply because he felt the urge. It is also worth noting that Mackay tried to attack another homeless man with a metal stake just one week after Heidi's murder. Furthermore, criminal psychologists point out that a serial killer's first murder is often the most sloppy and unlikely to fit the later pattern, because he is still establishing his method.

If Mackay did not commit the crime, someone else got away with Heidi Mnilk's murder. That person must have lacked control over his impulses, he must have been cold and calculating — because he followed Heidi to the empty carriage — and he must have been horribly violent. Given the apparent absence of similar murders around this time, he must have killed once and only once, or later become unlucky with his knife attacks. This killer was operating a few miles from where Mackay was living, he had strong feelings about Germany, a hatred of women and a blasé attitude towards covering his tracks. Two similar characters within spitting distance of each other is a huge coincidence.

A Family Destroyed —The Murders of Stephanie Britton and Christopher Martin

Just minutes from the busy North Circular Road and within the confines of the M25 motorway that encircles the capital, lies the affluent and leafy area of Hadley Green. Technically part of Barnet, North London, the well-to-do village is where the Big Smoke ends and the green fields of Hertfordshire begin. The otherwise tranquil village green is dissected by the Great North Road, which merges into Barnet High Street and then snakes down towards Finchley. On either side are several grand houses, set back from the main road behind rows of trees and three small ponds.

On Hadley Green Road sits The Mercers, one of the most impressive properties in the area. Worth £2.7m today, the house was built in 1953, a replacement for three cottages destroyed by Nazi bombs in 1944. The Mercers was named by its first owners, Mervyn Britton and his wife Stephanie, but the original cottages were known simply as Mercers, after a doctor who was the partner of Mrs Britton's father.

It was in this idyllic setting that one of the most heinous crimes of 1970s London was committed. Today, few people remember the horrific events that took place in that house more than four decades ago. When I visited the area, almost nobody had heard of the murders of Stephanie Britton, a 58-year-old widow, and her 4-year-old grandson Christopher Martin. Barely a word has been written about their deaths in the last forty years, until now.

There is no doubt that Stephanie Britton was well regarded in the community. The local newspaper at the time, the *Barnet Press*, published a glowing obituary, describing her as 'well known and held in such high esteem'. It continued:

> 'A quiet, modest woman of immense charm, Mrs Britton loved the less material things of life. She combined a lively personality with shrewdness, a sense of humour and a transparent sincerity which people responded to warmly. Her many special talents were used to enhance her own enjoyment of the arts and enrich the lives and experience of others. Her love for Hadley was something she felt intensely and it was reflected in the wide range of activities with which she was associated throughout her life, either officially or behind the scenes.'

Stephanie Britton was a Hadley Green girl through and through, having been born at the White House, a grand Georgian building, which stood at the top of Barnet High Street until it was knocked down to make way for a parade of shops. Her parents were the founders of Barnet Arts Club and Stephanie became an 'actress of outstanding ability' who also enjoyed designing costumes. She even roped her husband Mervyn, a successful solicitor, into the club. Her last turn on the stage was as a retired actress in Noel Coward's *Waiting in the Wings*.

Mervyn, a partner in the firm Longmores of Hertford, died in 1969 and Stephanie spent much of her time tending to her garden or doting on Christopher, the only son of her daughter Joanna Martin. She was also a member of the Barnet Old People's Welfare Committee and was treasurer of the Hadley Darby and Joan Club. Following her death, the local paper reported that she had been planning to downsize and put The Mercers on the market. But it wasn't to be.

Joanna went to collect Christopher from the house on 12 January 1974, as the youngster had stayed overnight. She was greeted by the sight of her mother lying dead in the lounge, a single knife wound to the chest. Frantically she searched for Christopher and found him dead in an upstairs bedroom, dressed in his pyjamas. He too had been stabbed in the chest. There was no sign of a forced entry but drawers in some of the rooms had been rifled through.

The police, led by DSUP W.G. Wilson of Scotland Yard, located a suspect immediately. He spent the best part of a week being questioned at Barnet Police Station, before being released on the Friday. The man was said to be 'helping police with their enquiries' but there was no suggestion he was ever arrested, and he was certainly never charged. In the meantime, detectives dredged the Hadley Green ponds in search of the suspected murder weapon — a double-edged stiletto knife. Officers appealed on the television show *Police Five* for anyone who had tried to contact Stephanie by phone on the day of the murder.

The following week a memorial service was held for Stephanie and Christopher at nearby Monken Hadley Church. Eddie Williams, a friend of the Brittons, told more than 300 mourners how Stephanie 'hated fuss', in a touching and at times amusing eulogy. 'You were fussing if you went to bed with a cold,' he told the congregation, 'and sentimentality was entirely foreign to her.' During the service, she was described as 'quietly spoken, gentle and ladylike' but with a 'resolution of iron'. Eddie Williams added: 'Every time we had a holiday or went to their house there was laughter. Perhaps I should not say it here, but her close friends will know what I mean when I say she had a very masculine sense of humour.'

By 1 February, police said they were looking for a 'tall, dark-haired man', about 30 years old, who was seen in the area at 8pm on the day of the murders. He was said to have short, straight hair and was wearing a 'long, dark, military topcoat' with a belt. That evening he was seen close to Joslin's Pond, the nearest pond to The Mercers, and at 5.30am the next day he was spotted walking away from the green towards Potters Bar.

Detectives called a number of people who had been seen in the area, including a group of schoolboys, to come forward and give statements. Police also changed their view on the murder weapon. Instead of a small stiletto blade, they were now looking for an ordinary single-edged kitchen knife. Later that became a nine-inch, wooden-handled carving knife.

On 15 February 1974, more than a month after the murders and the day after Isabella Griffiths, Mackay's first official victim (after the homeless man) was killed, police announced a significant new line of enquiry. DSUP Wilson revealed Stephanie may have invited someone into her home, or possibly left the door unlocked in anticipation of a visit.

'In the room where Mrs Britton was found — near the telephone — was a note saying, "Alan, I am on the telephone, please come in. Steph." We have interviewed five or six Alans but we should like to find the person who could recognize the note. Or someone who could tell us who Alan is,' said Wilson. He also revealed that a man and a woman had called New Scotland Yard from a phone box in Barnet, each saying they had information about the murders. But they hung up when asked for their names.

By this point, police had questioned one prime suspect and interviewed more than 1,000 people. 'Mrs Britton was so popular and active and so well known in the Barnet area, she must have known many people,' added Wilson. Meanwhile, Stephanie and her grandson were buried side by side at Bells Hill Burial Ground in Barnet.

Detectives considered Mackay to be a viable suspect after he was arrested for the murder of Father Crean. Once again, he had allegedly confessed to the crime while bragging to another inmate in Brixton Prison. However, he did not make a confession to police and vigorously denied he had anything to do with the double killing. He later wrote: 'It is my belief that they will always wonder whether I knew something about this bizarre slaying or not. The answer, of course, is that I did not.'

Nevertheless, once again, there was strong circumstantial evidence linking him to the crime. He was living in Finchley with Reverend Ted Brack at the time of the murders, just a few stops from Barnet on the Northern Line and easily reachable by bus. In fact, Mackay had been working for the furniture firm Perrings of Finchley, quitting just weeks earlier on 5 January 1974. The authors of *Psychopath* claimed Mackay admitted visiting The Mercers while on a job with the firm, but there is no indication of when that supposed visit took place. Absent from newspaper reports, but published in the book, were claims that Stephanie's front door was locked from the inside before the murderer left through the back, another clue suggesting Mackay's involvement.

But the authors of that book were not infallible. They also wrote that, at the time of the murders, Mackay had started work as a groundsman at the Tudor Sports Ground in Barnet, a job he would hold down for just eleven days. However, police records indicate he started on 14 January — two days after Stephanie and Christopher were killed. It is possible he visited the area before he started the job, either for a formal interview or while on a quest to find work. What is not in question is that Mackay was familiar with the area and he was unemployed and at a loose end for a period of at least nine days, during which the murders were committed.

After quitting the groundsman's job, Mackay spent four months working as a patrolling 'trustee' at Monken Hadley Common, just a few minutes' walk from the house where they were murdered. While in prison he was taken out to view The Mercers in an effort to jog his memory. Despite his familiarity with the area, he stuck to his denial and claimed not to recognize the house.

There are other elements of the crime that could suggest Mackay's involvement. Stephanie Britton was an archetypal Mackay victim. She was wealthy, a widow and she lived alone. She was also trusting; there was a note left for 'Alan' inviting him to come in because she was on the phone. Had she pinned it outside in advance or slipped it through the letter box when someone she knew called at the door? It could be possible that Mackay had struck up a friendly relationship with Stephanie while on business with the furniture firm, using the pseudonym 'Alan'. He had used the same method of gaining Isabella Griffiths' trust a year earlier. Even if the name 'Alan' is a red herring, Stephanie's trusting nature suggests that if Mackay had come calling she may well have let him in.

And what of the murder itself? Stephanie was killed with a single stab wound to the chest, pinning her to the floor. Isabella Griffiths was murdered with a knife blow to the chest while lying on the floor, after Mackay strangled her. Father Crean was also stabbed, as well as bludgeoned with an axe. Mackay's fondness for using knives — in particular with a blow to the chest — was well known.

Perhaps more suggestive are the sightings of the tall man in his 30s, seen near Joslin's Pond. He was apparently spotted at 8pm on 11 January and at 5.30am the following day, leaving a time frame of nine and a half hours, where he could have been inside the property. No attempt was made to dispose of the bodies or clean up the murder scene, so why would a potential killer have spent so long at the house? It is unlikely that a crime of passion would have resulted in such a pointless and lengthy stay — an enraged or panicked killer would either have fled the scene immediately or tried to cover his tracks. We know Mackay enjoyed being in the company of his dead victims for extended periods of time. After killing Isabella Griffiths, he dawdled in the kitchen, filling the sink with a number of items, including shoes, and exploring the previously off-limits areas of her home. Once he had dispatched Adele Price he stood at the French windows looking out on Lowndes Square, before switching on the radio and dozing off. He only left the flat when her granddaughter came home. After killing Father Crean, he spent up to an hour staring at the corpse, wandering around the cottage and 'doodling' in the garden. Did he fall asleep at The Mercers?

Four other key questions — Were taps run in the house? Were curtains closed? Were doors locked? Were the bodies covered in any way? — should have been applied to any suspected Patrick Mackay murder scene. It is impossible to answer them because the police files are still sealed. But a positive answer to at least one would strongly suggest Mackay's involvement.

However, the most glaring difference between this and Mackay's other crimes was the cold-blooded murder of the young boy. Killed by a single knife blow through the chest, Christopher Martin was just 4 years old and would have presented no threat to anyone. But Mackay had a history of unpredictable violence aimed at victims of different ages. Although he usually sought out vulnerable old women, he was prone to lash out whenever the 'mist' came down. If Mackay had previously scouted out The Mercers and Stephanie Britton as a potential robbery victim, he would not have known about the child staying the night. It's possible the boy was simply in the wrong place at the wrong time and was killed principally because it presented an opportunity for Mackay to take another life.

A further point to consider is that despite Stephanie's obvious wealth, very little — if anything — was stolen from the home. Perhaps this suggests a crime of passion. Or perhaps it points to a typical Mackay robbery-with-violence, where violence is the real end. Again, the question arises: if Mackay wasn't responsible for two murders bearing many hallmarks of his other crimes, who was?

I spoke to a member of Stephanie's family in November 2017 who asked not to be identified. Unlike Vic Davies, whose mother Ivy was murdered, he tries to avoid thinking about the killings and prefers to live with the trauma quietly, rather than worrying about who was responsible. He told me Joanna has since died, but he revealed that the family never believed the man originally questioned over the crime was the killer, and they were never told about any other suspects. He said police last reviewed the case in 2012, but nothing came of it.

'It isn't something I like to dwell on too often,' he told me. 'I can see why some people might but it's painful and I just don't see any prospect of it being solved now after all this time. There was a suggestion of a domestic motive but that is not something I have ever believed in. I know Patrick Mackay lived nearby and he was a serial killer. But it was only a few years after it happened that we were told he had been a suspect. Police investigations were very different then and we were told very little.'

The £5 Killer — The Murder of Sarah Rodmell

The elderly have been targeted repeatedly by serial killers. Kenneth Erskine, the Stockwell Strangler, was convicted of murdering seven pensioners although he probably killed more, and Dr Harold Shipman killed hundreds. Mackay killed at least two elderly victims — Isabella Griffiths and Adele Price — and spoke of longing to 'wipe out' old people in tribute to the Nazi's theories on eugenics. No doubt he also viewed 63-year-old Father Crean as elderly, although he would not be considered very old by today's standards. After his arrest for killing the priest, Mackay was questioned about one more murdered pensioner.

Sarah Rodmell, also known as Sarah Rodwell, was a 92-year-old spinster who spent most of her days drinking in a seedy East End boozer called the Temple Street Tap in Temple Street, Hackney. She would come in at opening time and leave when the bar closed, perching on the same stool and sipping from a bottle of Guinness. It may not have seemed a typical place for an elderly woman to frequent, especially as its main attractions were topless bar staff and 'go-go dancers' who gyrated all day long for the mainly male punters, but Sarah enjoyed the rowdy atmosphere and the dancers liked having her around. She was known for always wearing men's slippers, a flowerpot hat and a long black coat. Pub regulars gave her the nicknames 'Ginger' and 'Old Sarah'.

The pub, on the corner of Hackney Road and Temple Street, is now a block of flats. But on 23 December 1974, it was thriving. Sarah left the premises after her day's drinking and took a poorly-lit route home to Ash Grove, just north of the Thames. The journey took her along Hackney Road, left at The Oval, along a number of dark passages to Cambridge Heath Road and then Andrews Road, before she finally reached the Ash Grove cul-de-sac. Although she finished the journey unscathed, Sarah didn't make it through her front door. The following morning, she was found bludgeoned to death on her doorstep by neighbour Frank Couch.

In a part of London that has seen more than its fair share of violence, the murder of 'Old Sarah' stood out. Not only did it happen just before Christmas, therefore magnifying the tragedy, but the savagery of the attack was extreme, with police describing her head wounds as 'horrific' and revealing that her underwear had been 'disturbed'. Sarah had left the pub with just £5 in her purse. The purse had been stolen and now the local paper, the *Hackney Gazette*, dubbed her murderer 'The £5 Killer'.

Regulars at the Temple Street Tap were dismayed. Laura Harris, the licensee's wife, said Sarah was a 'sweet old lady' who was 'like a mother' to her. 'All the customers, young and old, loved her,' she said. 'On Sunday night, after we learned she had been killed, there was a terrible atmosphere in the pub. Everybody was upset. I dread to think what would happen to her attacker if any of our customers found out who it was.'

Dancer Paulette Blackman said, 'I was stunned and cried. Old Sarah used to sit there clapping me. She seemed to like the music and my dancing.' Pub regulars were later pictured in the paper after raising £160 to pay for her funeral and a headstone. Landlord Harry Harris said, 'We feel that she didn't have a decent death but are determined to see that she gets a decent funeral.' Harry spent several weeks making futile announcements over the pub's speaker system, appealing for information.

The investigation was led by DCSUP John Cass (who would later court controversy when, as commander, he wrote the report into the death of Blair Peach after he was hit by a police officer) and DI David Stephenson, head of Hackney's murder squad. Detectives soon established Sarah's route home and that she had stopped to rest on a wall under the railway bridge for up to half an hour. The walk was re-enacted by detective Daphne Robeson — who at 40 was less than half Sarah's age — more than two weeks after the murder. Dressed in a black flowerpot hat and coat, she stooped and shuffled along, clutching a handbag. Robeson left the pub at 11.10pm and was helped across the road by barman Brynley Gregory, just as he had done on the night of Sarah's murder. Passers-by who stopped to see what was going on were asked if they were in the area on that fateful night. Robeson put on a good act, but her efforts led to a mere trickle of information.

Two tip-offs were received by the local paper. One, from a man who claimed he had overheard a conversation in a pub discussing the murder. A second tipster left a first name for the suspected killer and an address. Cass said the tip-offs would be acted upon, although the *Hackney Gazette*'s poor-quality tape machine hindered progress.

'This is exactly the sort of thing we have been waiting for,' said Cass. 'The contents of the message are of considerable interest to us, but there is a certain amount of interference on the tape which prevents the message from being clearly heard.'

Another caller gave the name of a youth who was supposedly responsible, and said his mother was planning to smuggle him out of the country to Ireland. Detectives later said they were looking for a £1 note with the words 'Lou 1974' written on the back, which was thought to have been taken from Sarah's purse. But they didn't have much else to go on and the investigation petered out.

Mackay was later questioned, again after allegedly confessing to fellow prisoners. He managed to provide an alibi and in his memoir he simply wrote, 'She was found battered to death. I was never charged with that.'

So why did Mackay come under suspicion? The full extent of Sarah Rodmell's injuries were not published at the time, but she was bludgeoned repeatedly with a heavy object. It was a savage attack and no doubt detectives looked at the cases of Father Crean and Frank Goodman and felt there were obvious similarities.

At the time, Mackay was living in the bail hostel in the Great North Road, Holloway. He had been released from prison on 22 November after pleading guilty to possession of an offensive weapon (a metal stake with which he had tried to attack a homeless man). We know that he spent Christmas Day drinking with a friend at the hostel, and robbed Lady Becher at her home in Belgravia on Boxing Day. Could he have ventured to Hackney, a forty-minute journey on London's train system two days earlier?

Hackney, in East London, was not one of his regular stalking grounds, but there is every likelihood that he visited the area. Interestingly, Rev Ted Brack was known to drink in the Lord Hood pub in Bethnal Green, which was a twenty-minute walk from Sarah's home. It is quite possible that he drank there and Mackay accompanied him and got to know the area. In any case, he hardly needed the company of a vicar to roam London. He would habitually drift from pub to pub and it is entirely plausible that he spent time in the Temple Street Tap that evening and stalked his prey at closing time.

The choice of Sarah Rodmell as a victim was, on the face of it, out of keeping with Mackay's usual targets. She was by no means wealthy — the £5 stolen from her purse was her pensioner's Christmas bonus. And the murder took place outside her house in a somewhat frenzied fashion. Mackay preferred to gain access to the property so he could commit his crimes in private. The apparent sexual element also did not match his modus operandi. However, Sarah Rodmell's stockings had been 'disturbed' and it is not clear whether this meant semen was found at the scene or they had been pulled at, in an attempt to remove them to create a ligature. Mackay alluded to using stockings in crimes even though he was never convicted of such an offence.

Once again his unpredictability has to be a factor. He was blind drunk that Christmas and committed a number of offences, including the robbery of Lady Becher. He was estranged from his family, shunned by Rev Brack, unemployed and entirely at a loose end. Following the hypotheses that Sarah was followed home from the pub, it is worth considering that the Temple Street Tap would have been one of the closest pubs to Cambridge Heath Railway Station. Like so many of the crimes associated with Mackay, a public transport link was less than a five-minute walk away.

A Seaside Mystery — The Murder of Ivy Davies

The brutal death of café owner Ivy Davies has already been explored in the opening chapter. Like Father Crean, Frank Goodman and Sarah Rodmell, she was repeatedly battered around the head with a heavy object at her home in Westcliff,

Essex, on 3 February 1975. But how did Mackay end up in the frame for a crime committed so far from home?

Like so many other cases, he apparently admitted the murder while in prison. But there was no evidence in the files I reviewed that Mackay had ever visited Essex, let alone Southend or Westcliff. It is clear, however, that he could have been a suspect in almost any murder by stabbing, strangulation or bludgeoning committed between his release from Moss Side and his arrest for the murder of Father Crean in April 1975, as long as it was carried out within a reasonable public transport commuting distance from London.

While Mackay committed the bulk of his crimes in upmarket Kensington and Chelsea, he had also travelled out to his mother's home in Kent by train before making his way to Father Crean's home on foot. Ivy Davies' home was a similar distance from London and just a two-minute walk from Westcliff Railway Station. The unsolved cases of Mary Hynes and Frank Goodman — for which Mackay was charged but not prosecuted — also took place within minutes of public transport links. Heidi Mnilk was killed on a train, while Sarah Rodmell was more than likely stalked from a pub just minutes from the area's main train station. Was the close proximity of Westcliff Station a factor in Ivy's murder? A young male, who was never identified, was seen walking in that direction the morning her body was found.

Ivy's son, Vic, told me detectives said Mackay had signed on the dole in Southend during the week of his mother's murder, because he was there on holiday. Vic claims they told him Mackay's documented presence in the town was the reason they took his prison confession so seriously. But apart from the fact that a holiday didn't particularly fit Mackay's chaotic and unpredictable lifestyle, there is an even more prosaic reason to question his involvement.

As we know, Mackay confessed to carrying out one of his doorstep robberies in Red Lion Square, Holborn, on the day Ivy was killed. DSUP John Bland almost forgot to ask him about it and took it 'out of rotation' during questioning. After the robbery, Mackay made off from the scene with an inscribed silver pen. But he also walked off with something he could not have appreciated at the time — an alibi, or at least enough of an alibi to create doubts that he also committed a crime in Essex on the same day.

It is still possible Mackay boarded a train to Essex that afternoon, stumbling drunk out of Westcliff Station. He may have walked down towards the seafront, spotting Ivy Davies as she put her key in the lock. There were certainly elements of Ivy's murder that pointed to Mackay's involvement. For instance, there was no sign of a forced entry. While this could suggest Ivy knew her killer, it could also mean someone forced their way in as she opened the door, or that they tricked their way inside. There was no sign of a struggle, just as there had been no struggle when Mackay killed Isabella Griffiths and Adele Price.

Ivy was battered around the head with a heavy metal object, a pry bar which police said was shaped like an axe. The weapon was discarded just a few feet away from the body in a curtained alcove. It had echoes of the way Mackay returned the bloody axe he used to kill Father Crean to the spot under the stairs where he found it. It was also reminiscent of the screwdriver he left behind in Adele Price's flat and the way he carelessly disposed of evidence in other crimes. Additionally, very little, if anything, was taken of value. For such a brutal crime, remarkably little effort was made to profit from it.

The fact that a ligature was found around Ivy's neck seemed to point away from Mackay. He had strangled Isabella Griffiths and Adele Price with his bare hands. There is no evidence he ever used a ligature on anyone other than himself, while he was locked up in a psychiatric hospital. But he made an odd comment while being interviewed over the Adele Price killing. When asked about a nylon stocking found at the scene, he told detectives, 'No, I don't think I did, but if it was there it would appear I must have used it. I may have used it to tie around the woman's neck but I don't think I did. I used my hands. That would be the only reason I would use a nylon stocking.'

While this could have been a reference to the stocking stuffed in the mouth of Mary Hynes after she was killed, or the stockings 'disturbed' on Sarah Rodmell, it might have referred to Ivy Davies. There is a further similarity to the Isabella Griffiths killing, in that the attempted strangulation was not actually the cause of death.

Other key questions remain unanswered. It is not known whether Ivy's door keys were removed after her murder. Madeline, her daughter's friend, had to use her key to get in, suggesting the door may have been locked. There is also no record of whether the curtains were drawn.

Mackay covered the legs of Isabella Griffiths, closed the eyes of Adele Price and placed a towel over Father Crean's head. Frank Goodman had been covered, and there was an attempt to place Mary Hynes on the bed before her legs were covered with an eiderdown. Was anything placed over Ivy's legs or head after she died? And did she die on the sofa or was she placed there? Vic told me the wounded side of his mother's head was positioned face down, so the injuries could not immediately be seen. This could suggest an attempt to hide the wounds, as Mackay had done after killing Father Crean, because he felt they did not look 'nice'. Bar being given access to Essex Police's records, there is no accurate way of knowing.

According to *Psychopath*, Mackay did admit to visiting Southend in 1972 and said he had considered robbing Ivy Davies. If true, it was certainly a coincidence that a woman a serial killer had once thought of victimizing had now been murdered. Mackay didn't agree, as he wrote in his memoir: 'At the request of the Southend police we went to view this murder house. She had apparently been hit one killing blow on the head. I was never charged with this and I would think not too. It certainly wasn't me they wanted.'

* * *

With a lack of evidence, the investigation petered out. There were no developments of any significance until 2005, a year after Crimestoppers offered a reward for information.

Ray Newman, a former detective who worked on Essex Police's major crimes review team at the time, told me a 'trickle' of information started to come in after the 2004 appeal, none of it of any substance. But in February 2005, he received a call from Vic Davies. He had been given the name of a potential witness who Newman was eventually able to contact. The woman described how a man, who lived near Ivy at the time but who now lived in nearby Basildon, had visited Ivy's house and made a pass at her. When Ivy rebuffed his advances he lashed out with the pry bar. Covered in blood, he crept back to his own house via a series of back gardens. He confessed to his partner and she returned with him to Ivy's house to make the scene look like a burglary gone wrong.

Newman checked the case files. All the people named by the woman had been questioned during the original investigation, but no action was taken. The case was passed to the Rayleigh Major Investigation Team, headed by DSUP Simon Dinsdale and a full investigation was launched. Officers visited Ivy's old neighbours, including Stella Zammitt, one of the women who had discovered Ivy's body. It transpired that after her death some of Ivy's belongings were divided among her friends and unbelievably, this included carpet from the living room stained with Ivy's blood. It was still rolled up in Mrs Zammitt's attic. Forensics officers examined the carpet and found a semen stain.

The suspect, then aged 68, was arrested. However, initial hopes that police might be able to bring a charge were dashed when tests on the carpet came up blank. The man was released with no further action. Simon Dinsdale spoke to me in August 2017 about the Ivy Davies case — but he seemed puzzled by my questions about Mackay.

'He was a figure in the investigation,' he said. 'But I don't remember reading any interviews with him or anything about him coming to view the house. It wasn't our focus. He was some kind of vagrant who had been ruled out.'

Ray Newman didn't recall much about Mackay either. He was just one of many men questioned over Ivy's death. One former detective involved in the early stages of the original investigation — former DC Dave Bright — told me he couldn't remember anything about Mackay, despite the case having a personal meaning for him. Ivy's café, the Orange Tree, was frequented by police and not just because of its quality breakfast: 'A lot of the local villains would sit there and have a cup of coffee or tea every morning and discuss their business,' he said. 'They all knew we were police officers, it's one of the ways we cultivated contacts. We all knew Ivy because she used to serve us breakfast too. As far as we were concerned she was a very nice lady and when she was murdered we felt like it had happened on our turf.'

Both reviewing detectives felt it unlikely that Mackay was ever spoken to again by Essex Police after 1975, and his DNA was not tested against the carpet sample found in 2005. Neither officer could remember the details of the ligature found around Ivy's neck, whether the door was locked after the murder, whether taps had been run, whether the curtains had been closed or whether anything had been placed over her body.

This is by no means a criticism of either man — both diligent and committed detectives — because their job was only to investigate the new information. But their accounts are helpful because they suggest other Mackay-related cold cases may well have been treated the same way.

For a short while in 2017, Patrick Mackay seemed to be back in the frame. At least according to the story Vic had relayed to me on the phone, that of the new witness who came forward and told Vic she was working at the Orange Tree when Ivy was murdered. She had claimed a man had visited the café with a group of other men, stating that he was a doctor from the nearby Runwell Mental Hospital, in Wickford, taking some patients on a day trip. Ivy apparently agreed to meet the doctor for a date on Southend seafront. The man later turned up unannounced at Ivy's home, a practice that was verboten, according to Vic. The new witness said it later transpired that the men in the café — including the doctor — were 'escaped mental patients'. Vic said he remembered something like this happening because everybody subsequently mocked Ivy for her gullibility, but nobody could remember exactly when the incident had taken place. It could have been weeks or even months before her murder. If Vic could remember it happening, it must have been several weeks at least, because he was locked up in borstal shortly before his mother's death. However, the woman told Vic the 'doctor' gave his name as Patrick Mackay, or something similar.

Could there have been any truth to the claim? The witness said the escapee scandal had been 'hushed up' by the embarrassed authorities and there was no mention of any such incident in the local newspapers. All I could find were stories about a scandal of a different nature at the hospital — bosses had been allowing staff to have 'sleepovers' with male friends. I contacted several former Runwell employees and nobody could remember anything about a mass escape. Neither could they remember a man named Patrick Mackay. Nothing in his medical records suggested Mackay had ever been a patient at Runwell, although it is possible he checked himself in under a pseudonym. He often gave false names, not only to his victims, but to police and doctors. However, in the complete absence of any evidence, we cannot say Mackay was ever a patient at Runwell.

That is not to say Mackay never *claimed* to be at Runwell. He would often tell his London victims about his treatment at Tooting Bec. He would also lie, saying he was an inpatient and he had to return soon, when he had in fact absconded or had not been seen at the hospital for months. If Mackay was in Essex, he might have lied about having connections with the local psychiatric hospital, in this case Runwell. He might have said he was a patient there, or even a doctor.

There is another possible explanation — the witness simply got it wrong. She was only about 14 at the time. She might have heard the man mention something about a psychiatric hospital. It could have been Tooting Bec or Moss Side, but she may have assumed the hospital in question was the local one, Runwell. There is also considerable doubt about when this alleged incident took place. As there is no evidence of Mackay visiting Southend shortly before Ivy's murder, did this exchange take place back in 1972, when he claimed to have visited the town and contemplated robbing Ivy Davies? A further explanation is that the escaped patient scenario never took place, or it took place in a very different way to how she remembers. In any case, Essex Police spoke to the woman in summer 2017. When I asked them if Mackay would be interviewed as a result of what she said, I was told he would not. The woman herself, who still lives in Southend, declined to be interviewed for this book.

I met with Vic Davies in May 2018. He told me he had begged Essex Police to arrange a meeting between Mackay and himself, but he was told it would be impractical and whatever Mackay said would not necessarily be admissible in court. Vic was frustrated by the lack of action and partly blamed the stress of the case on a heart attack he had suffered seven months earlier.

Yet despite being intrigued by the possibility of Mackay's involvement, he still harboured suspicions about the two young men who had been questioned in 1975, and the couple quizzed in 2005.

'I don't know what to think and I'm not sure I will ever get an answer now,' he told me. 'Unless it's a deathbed confession. But that's really no good to me. If someone admits it when they're about to die anyway, it still means they got away with it.'

Chapter 10

Wasted Forever to Rot

Despite being one of Britain's most brutal and sadistic serial killers, Patrick Mackay was destined to fade into relative obscurity. In hindsight, it is easy to see why. Although there were many missed opportunities to stop Mackay's crime spree, once detectives had the suspect in their sights they wasted no time in taking him off the streets. As a result, there was no well-publicized manhunt and no great fanfare when he was arrested and then charged. At the time, the general public and even victims' families were kept in the dark about the serious questions being asked in custody. Even when Mackay appeared in public, for a hearing at the Old Bailey on 21 November 1975, it was a short-lived affair, compared with the high-profile trials of serial murderers Peter Sutcliffe and Dennis Nilsen.

It was only a few days before his court appearance that the *London Evening Standard* published the first photograph of Mackay, with the caption: 'This is the face of the man police say is London's five-time murderer — the man who is alleged to have brought fear to Belgravia and Chelsea's Cheyne Walk.' The report said his trial was expected to be short, following discussions between defence and prosecution lawyers. The implication was that a deal had been made.

On 7 November Mackay wrote in his prison journal about the upcoming court appearance. 'I shan't shed a tear,' he wrote. 'Life is full of shocks of all descriptions and they have to be faced. I am now informed that my trial will be later this month. So I await my destiny. I hope from this writing someone somewhere, wherever it may be read, will pick up some good from my experiences. I am just one example of many bad ones. But who can say totally so?'

In the end, there was no trial. Arriving at court in a new black suit, paid for by his lawyer, and sitting placidly in the dock for much of the hearing, Mackay made little impression. The *Daily Mail* described the courtroom scene, with Mackay surrounded by six burly security guards, looking 'tall and gaunt' and 'wearing the faintest of beards'. He spoke only when repeating the words of his lawyer, Michael Parker QC: 'Not guilty to murder, guilty to manslaughter on the grounds of diminished responsibility.' In the end, he only had to repeat the phrase three times because the Mary Hynes and Frank Goodman cases were left to lie on file.

The packed court listened for an hour as details of Mackay's crimes and confessions were read out. An extract from his prison memoir, relating to the killing of Isabella Griffiths, was reported in most of the papers. He wrote:

'She was not a bad soul, and why I killed her I feel I may never know. I suppose that even though I had killed her, I wanted in death to make her comfortable as she lay on her kitchen floor. I closed her eyes as they were staring lifeless up, covered her as if in a sleeping bag and left her there. These murders were so solemn when I think of them, yet so quick, so fast to take place. You know, a man who has killed cannot really say much more than the basics from his point of view as he remembers it. In my case, for instance, I became very cocky about a few things that happened. It has been said that I must have closed all the curtains in the homes of my victims as they say. This may well be possible. I have never disputed it. But I cannot say this with any certainty for I just do not recall so doing. There is a hell of a lot from the point of view of these killings that I cannot myself remember.'

The role of Mackay's lawyer was not to get his client to plead innocent, but to convince the judge that he could be dealt with by a hospital order. Mackay himself had written a note begging to be sent to the high-security psychiatric hospital Broadmoor and in his memoir he gave the reasons why:

'The doctors whom I have seen feel that I may not or would not respond to medical help if it were to be given or offered to me. It is in fact the direct opposite. I would be willing body and soul to accept medical help in a secure hospital for many years to come if necessary, for I know deep down that this is just what I need if there is to be any future for me to lead a normal life. I believe that nowhere else except Broadmoor can I get the help I need. I must be helped. I cannot remain in the state I am for the rest of my life. It is my last hope to survive as a human being.'

But his hopes were dashed when the Old Bailey heard from Dr Peter Scott, a consultant psychiatrist at the Home Office, who assessed him on 26 March, just days after his arrest. He said Mackay had 'well-marked sadistic interests' in Nazis and dictators and reported that during an interview, Mackay had made the chilling confession that 'any man doing a killing enjoys it at the time – it's animal.' The doctor insisted he could not be treated at a secure hospital because of the risk to other patients and staff. 'He has displayed a persistent disorder disability of mind, which has resulted in abnormally aggressive behaviour,' he said. 'Mackay was described by a doctor at Ashford Remand Centre as a cold psychopathic killer.'

His view was backed up by Professor Trevor Gibbons of the Royal College of Psychiatrists. He told the court Mackay had an 'extreme form of personality disorder known as psychopathic personality' and could not be treated. 'What to do with this man presents considerable problems,' he said. 'He is a risk to himself and the inmates and the staff of whatever institution he is likely to be in. In the circumstances, I recommend detention indefinitely in a prison, and if he were to start that sentence in a prison hospital wing it might be possible at a later date to transfer him to a secure hospital if that proved necessary.'

When it was time to be sentenced, Mackay stood to attention in the dock as Mr Justice Milmo handed him three life sentences, with a minimum of twenty years and a warning that he may never be released. 'You are a highly dangerous man and it is my duty to protect the public,' said the judge gravely. 'That I can only do by making an order which will ensure that unless and until you cease to be the menace you now are, you will be kept in secure custody.' Mackay was led down to the cells and taken to Parkhurst Prison, one of several jails he would later call home.

Every national newspaper splashed on the case. 'Life for the mad killer the law let go,' screamed the *Daily Mail*. The *Daily Mirror* dubbed Mackay 'The Devil's Disciple', while *The Sun* called him a 'fiend', the 'psycho who had to kill' and 'The Monster of Belgravia'.

During the trial, anyone who'd had the misfortune to know Mackay had been targeted by journalists and now sentencing was complete, the press was free to publish their interviews. Bert and Vi Cowdrey had been called upon to explain what they knew. The couple posed outside their home in Stockwell with the two-foot Nazi eagle Mackay had stored there, along with photos of Mussolini and Hitler. 'He loved war films and would go to them all the time,' said Bert. 'He also liked to go to war museums. We never really got to know him. But we knew he could be very violent when he was drunk, and he became restless at night time. He always had to go out. Now we know what for. I knew he was a tormented young man with mental troubles. It was very scary and we didn't know then what it was all about.' Vi called Mackay a 'split personality' and added, 'during the day he was full of laughs.'

Mackay's former neighbours in Gravesend also spoke out, insisting the authorities had ignored their pleas to remove him from the area. 'Patrick was a real tearaway,' said one. Summing up the whole saga, he added: 'He would beat the hell out of his family but nobody seemed to do anything about it. There is not a person in the street who has not called the police at some time or other about him. He has been taken away in a straightjacket after beating up his mother, and then 24 hours later he came waltzing down the road as free as a bird. The authorities literally gave him a licence to kill.'

Even Reverend Ted Brack spoke to journalists, although on condition of anonymity. When he was mentioned in the *Psychopath* book a year later, he was given the pseudonym Tom Black.

The nature of the short hearing and the decision to abandon two murder prosecutions left many questions unanswered, particularly about the other unsolved cases. The next day, photographs of some of Mackay's suspected victims — Heidi Mnilk, Stephanie Britton, Christopher Martin, Frank Goodman and Ivy Davies — were splashed over the news. Journalists also speculated about the unnamed homeless man, Mary Hynes and Sarah Rodmell.

An unnamed detective told *The Sun*, 'At one stage we thought we had a mass murderer with as many as ten or eleven victims. It looked as if we were going to clear our books of almost every outstanding murder in the London area. An oddball like Mackay, who kills for no reason, always presents the most difficult type of investigation. There is no doubt that he was one of the most dangerous and terrifying killers to be walking around London for a long time.' Meanwhile, the *Daily Mail* noted that Mackay's mother still refused to accept her son was evil and claimed he was a 'good boy'.

Yet it wasn't the mystery of Mackay's crimes that provoked the most outrage, it was the truly baffling circumstances in which he had been repeatedly freed to kill. During his eighteen-month crime spree, Mackay had been taken into psychiatric units twice and on both occasions released in under a week. Within days of each release he had killed someone.

It also emerged that before Mackay was discharged from the South Western Hospital in Lambeth, three days before killing Father Crean, Moss Side Hospital had told doctors it had no record of Patrick Mackay or his alias Peter McCann. This blunder no doubt contributed to the decision to release him.

In the aftermath of the case, Dr Robert Porter, who had been the deputy medical superintendent at Moss Side during Mackay's forced residency, told how he had fought the lay review tribunals instigated by Marion Mackay each time they came up. 'I felt both times that he needed much more care and training,' he said. 'I advised the tribunals not to release him on the basis of the evidence we had. It's all that could be done. As a psychiatrist, I feel that these types of people are not given a long enough course of training. This man needed longer.' Perhaps diplomatically, Dr Porter made no mention of the intense lobbying from Mackay's mother that had helped to secure the killer's release. 'The mental health tribunals have a difficult job,' he added.

Writing in the *Daily Mail*, Dr Donald Gould, a professor of psychology, said the mistakes made in the Mackay case were 'incredible'. He added:

> 'The first thing to say is that it would be grossly
> unfair to lay all the blame on the doctors and other
> people directly concerned with the individual case.

Patrick Mackay is a psychopath. He suffers from a defect of the mind, which allows him to respond in a totally uncontrolled fashion to the kind of animal instincts which we all have. A psychopath who is irritated by the hairstyle or mannerisms of somebody he meets — even a total stranger — may kill that person. He is not restrained by conscience, or by pity, or by any regard to the consequences to himself or others of his act. He is a person of normal, or even superior, intelligence. There is nothing to distinguish him from his fellow men.'

Dr Gould pointed out that psychiatrists do not have 'absolute power' over people brought into psychiatric institutions, but suggested that in future no 'proved psychopath' should ever be released unless they can be supervised 'for the rest of his life'.

The furore was such that the Conservative MP for Macclesfield, Nicholas Winterton, suggested some members of the Moss Side tribunal should face criminal charges. 'The people who released him and enabled him to commit these further crimes should be indicted for what has been done,' he demanded. 'They have caused the deaths of other innocent people.'

His colleague for Edgbaston, Jill Knight, urged action from the Home Secretary and added:

> 'Members of these tribunals ought to share the guilt for the people who were subsequently killed. This is a classic example of precisely why the general public are caught in a rising tide of fury at the total inability of the authorities to afford them normal protection in their daily lives. The cult of "be kind to the criminal and shower blessings on the violent" has been responsible for the deaths or injury of countless people in the last decade. Unless the government and the authorities recognize public

feeling in this matter, they will find themselves faced with the emergence of vigilante bands. I am extremely anxious that no such bands should erupt as it can only make the violence worse.'

No such 'vigilante bands' ever materialized, but while Mrs Knight's diatribe might be viewed as somewhat extreme, there was good reason for the politicians' fury. Three years earlier, the poisoner Graham Young had been jailed for life after murdering two workmates at the John Hadland Laboratories in Bovingdon, Hertfordshire. Known as the 'Teacup Poisoner' or 'St Alban's Poisoner', like Mackay, Young was influenced by the horrors committed by Nazis, had suffered trauma at a young age and attacked numerous members of his family, which resulted in him being locked up in Broadmoor for almost eight years. Considered to be 'fully recovered', he was freed and went on to kill two people and poison many others. The Young case led to the 1975 Butler Report on Britain's approach to mentally ill criminals, which prompted changes to the psychiatric hospital system, with a number of secure units opening up across the country. It also recommended removing the term 'psychopathy' from the Mental Health Act and replacing it with 'personality disorder' because of the difficulties associated with diagnosis, but this was not done until 2007.

Nevertheless, the Mackay case did not spark a high-profile inquiry and nobody lost their jobs as a result. Following his sentencing, his name would be heard in court on just one occasion, this time in connection with an equally bizarre and horrific murder case for which he was not actually responsible.

What happened during the trial of child killer Stanley Rogers is a perfect example of Mackay's manipulative nature and a fitting footnote to his short-lived career in the public eye. Rogers was at the Old Bailey charged with killing a 10-year-old girl, Alison Chadwick. She disappeared from Isleworth, Middlesex in June 1974 but her body was not found until

February the following year. Her tiny frame had been stuffed in a sack and dumped in a skip. Rogers, a 56-year-old labourer, was arrested and remanded in Brixton Prison, where he crossed paths with Mackay.

The psychopath was busy telling anyone who would listen about his long history of murder and mayhem, and that gave Rogers an idea. Through an intermediary — an Indian journalist called Sethi who was locked up in the prison's hospital wing — Rogers made an offer.

Prosecutors described the alleged deal in the following terms: Rogers would pay Mackay £15,000 in cash followed by £20 a week for fifteen years if he admitted murdering Alison Chadwick. Sethi apparently suggested the deal could be made legally binding by a solicitor and Rogers duly sent Mackay a bundle of police papers and handwritten notes so he could get his story straight. But Mackay decided to turn the tables. He wanted £2,000 in cash immediately, otherwise he would hand the notes to the police, potentially damning Rogers at a future trial. When the case did go before a jury in February 1976, the prosecutor, Kenneth Richardson, called Mackay's double cross 'a bit of blackmail'.

Rogers told a different version of events. He pleaded 'definitely not guilty' before trying to pin the blame on Mackay. He claimed Mackay had told him, 'I think I killed this child. I am thinking of going to the police and telling them the whole story.' Rogers insisted he told Mackay he didn't care what he did. Nevertheless, he claimed Sethi had taken it upon himself to try and broker a deal, coming up with the sum of £30,000. Rogers was acquitted of murder but found guilty of manslaughter. He was jailed for just twelve years. The exact cause of Alison's death could not be determined.

Although there was never any question of Mackay's involvement in the little girl's death, the fact the deal between Rogers and Mackay was even on the table speaks volumes about his behaviour. It is possible he did say the words attributed to him by Rogers. After all, he had already confessed to killing

Ivy Davies, Heidi Mnilk, Stephanie Britton, Christopher Martin and Sarah Rodmell while inside and detectives were taking those claims seriously. Yet there was nothing about the murder of Alison Chadwick that made Mackay a likely suspect. She was far too young for a typical Mackay victim, Middlesex was considerably out of the way, and her body was not found for several months because of a conscious effort to conceal her. It simply wasn't Mackay's style. Still, it didn't stop him from trying to benefit from the tragedy.

* * *

Patrick Mackay is now 66 years old and one of Britain's longest serving prisoners. But has prison changed him? And is there any chance he could someday be released?

Although the Mackay case has, until now, remained relatively obscure, there are two widely held misinterpretations of how it ended, which persist to this day. The first is that he has spent the last four decades being treated in Broadmoor. This is not true, because at his trial the judge ruled it inappropriate to hold him in a psychiatric hospital. The second is that he will certainly die in jail.

Although Mackay is said to have been given a 'whole life tariff' at his 1975 sentencing, the ability to impose such a sentence was not introduced until 1983. Even then, only the Home Secretary could order the measure. Mackay was instead given a life sentence for each count of manslaughter.

Since 1995, Mackay's case has appeared before the Parole Board on ten occasions. The most recent was in March 2017 — under his new name David Groves — where a decision was made to keep him in prison. However, the board also ruled that he was suitable to serve the rest of his sentence in a Category D facility, more commonly known as an open prison. The Ministry of Justice declined to comment on his status, and at the time of writing I have been unable to find out where Mackay is currently imprisoned. But he was due to have a further parole hearing in the summer of 2019. If the move to an open prison has now gone ahead, it could pave the way for his eventual release.

Writing in his prison memoir even before his sentencing, Mackay could see himself spending the rest of his life in prison:

> 'My life was wasted. I now realise that it is now wasted forever to rot. Something terrible had to come along in order to reveal the decaying disaster that my life has been since 1962. You know, when I look at myself now I could put a bullet through my head and through my brain for the kind of bloody life that I have had, but I do not know who would do me that service. I have often thought to myself, whenever I am alone, that it would be the best thing I could ever have done.'

There was no hint of remorse, no regret for what he had done to his victims, only at how it had affected him. Lack of empathy is a core trait of psychopathy, and it is highly unlikely Mackay has gained further insight over the years.

The clearest proof of his overall lack of progress came almost thirty years ago in 1989, when Mackay made a surprising appearance on an episode of the BBC documentary *40 Minutes* entitled Danger Men. It focused on an experimental unit in Hull Prison to deal with ten of the nation's most 'dangerous and disruptive' inmates. Described as a 'softly-softly' regime, the heavily-staffed unit cost about £1million. The idea was prison staff would not argue or fight with prisoners, but allow them to behave badly until they came round to the idea of having a conversation about their problems. It was a controversial proposition, particularly among staff.

One inmate, David McAllister, an armed robber serving nineteen years, escaped three weeks after the film was made, following an affair with a prison teacher. She had smuggled a gun into jail to help with his breakout, but the pair ended up strolling through the gates together unchallenged. He was captured and had eight years added to his sentence. Another contributor was Fred Lowe, infamous for killing two inmates in separate attacks at Gartree and Long Lartin prisons after originally being handed two life sentences for robbery and grievous bodily harm. The regime was so relaxed at the unit that the psychotic Lowe was allowed to prepare food and walk around the wing carrying knives. Violent heavyweight boxer and robber Paul Sykes — well-known for attacking prison officers — was also serving time on the unit.

The film starts with the then 39-year-old Patrick Mackay being led into the prison in handcuffs as the narrator tells how he and the others have been in 'constant trouble'. At the time of filming, Mackay had been taken from the segregation block at Parkhurst, the same jail that housed Graham Young and Ian Brady. Sporting a neat, combed-back hairstyle and tidy moustache, Mackay takes in his surroundings as he is led into the building. He has the air of a man checking out a potential new apartment, undecided about the suitability of the accommodation.

The robber McAllister is Mackay's cellmate and is seen helping him carry his artwork and equipment into his cell. Mackay is then shown chatting with another murderer, who asks him if he's ever been in Albany Prison on the Isle of Wight. In a soft voice, Mackay replies, 'Yes, I was at Albany in 1986 I think, for a short period of time. I wasn't there too long actually, I didn't particularly like the…I got there just after the riots.' Clearly, Mackay had lost none of his grandiose sense of self-worth and gave the impression he could pick and choose where he resided.

The documentary later shows Mackay chatting with the unit governor who asks whether he believes he was behaving 'psychopathically' during his killing spree. Despite plenty of doctors diagnosing him as a psychopath, numerous references to his condition in his prison memoir and comments made to psychiatrists about how he enjoyed killing, Mackay denied he was a psychopath. 'From the point of view of somebody who is supposedly using that label to enjoy taking human life, there was never, ever any suggestion in my mind that I was ever a psychopath, if one was to use that criteria,' he said. 'I could have perhaps understood some people being rather uncertain as to whether or not I was, but I certainly have never considered myself psychopathic, if one takes the criteria that one gets a special enjoyment out of killing. No such enjoyment have I ever had. I have never found any pleasure out of any such thing.'

Mackay is also shown at an induction meeting with prison officers, where he is told to settle in gradually and that he could still be on the unit in a year's time. Asked if the other inmates have given him any problems, Mackay shakes his head and says, 'No. Not as yet anyway, to be accurate.' When asked if he has concerns that there might be, he adds, 'Not particularly, no. But I can't read the future.'

While it is not known what happened later at Hull Prison, Mackay is known to have clashed with inmates during his incarceration. His enemies have included Britain's most notorious prisoner Charles Bronson, who wrote of Mackay in one of his books: 'Some days we would get lucky and catch him in the shower. He never once fought back. He just screamed like a little girl, rolling into a ball on the floor. Up against an 80-year-old woman he was Tarzan, oh yes, a big, brave fucker. Facing a man, he was a pussy.'

Could it be that Mackay's softly-spoken eloquence, his ability to get along with difficult prisoners and a perception that he had been bullied helped to convince the Parole Board he was safe to move to an open prison?

Another thing that may have helped is his love of art — the one constant in his life and a positive influence during his prison years. The BBC film shows Mackay making a clay sculpture while being observed by guards, and his work has been viewed by the public during exhibitions showcasing prisoners' art — always anonymously.

During the first half of this decade, Mackay was moved to HM Prison Wayland, a Category C prison in Norfolk, a sure sign the authorities felt his most dangerous and disruptive days were well and truly over. There, he created an impressive mural depicting an idyllic English village, with a rat-infested sewer system underneath, in a prisoners' communal area. One former inmate I spoke to described him as a 'quiet, model prisoner' who was 'focused on his art'. Yet his paintings did contain dark imagery as the inmate added, 'We had a theory that one of his paintings pointed to an unsolved murder.'

Could Mackay ever be released? The layman might think the Parole Board would have to consider whether he has admitted to all his crimes, but that is not necessarily the case. Although this book has never tried to pin the blame on Mackay for crimes he was not convicted of, he almost certainly murdered Frank Goodman and, if not for the bizarre situation around Ashford Remand Centre, there would be little doubt that he also killed Mary Hynes. It would be incredible if Mackay was not responsible for at least some of the other murders listed in this book. But a criminal can hardly be blamed for not confessing to a crime if the police are unable to bring charges, and consideration of the unsolved crimes could be out of the Parole Board's remit. This was seen recently in the case of 'Black Cab Rapist' John Worboys: the Parole Board approved his release with stringent license conditions but a legal challenge overruled it.

As a direct result of early publicity for this book in April 2019, the case of Patrick Mackay was raised in Parliament. Dartford's MP Gareth Johnson also met with Justice Minister David Gauke and wrote to Metropolitan Police Commissioner Cressida Dick, imploring her to re-open the unsolved cases.

Now would be the ideal time for police to re-examine these decades-old mysteries. Evidence shows that several of the probes into Mackay's confessions either fell short or have never been fully re-investigated by cold case teams. It is certainly the case with the murder of Ivy Davies because when new forensic evidence came to light, it was not tested with Mackay in mind. Even when a new witness came forward, detectives decided not to question him again.

There is also the possibility that updated forensic techniques could be applied to other cases. Scientists found no match for blood stains found on Mackay's grey Gabardine coat, which was recovered from his mother's home, but they were only testing them against samples from Father Crean. Where is that coat now and do police have other items of his clothing that could be tested again?

The fundamental problem of all the unsolved cases is that they were investigated by separate teams. The extent to which they shared information with each other cannot be known, but there is nothing in the paperwork I have seen to suggest there was much overlap. This lack of collaboration may have left important lines of questioning unexplored.

For instance, when asked about stockings during the interview over the death of Adele Price, Mackay said the only reason he would use them would be to strangle someone. The comment meant little to the interviewer, John Bland, because Mackay was not accused of using a stocking in the killings of Isabella Griffiths or Adele Price. But it could have been significant to officers investigating the murders of Mary Hynes, Ivy Davies and Sarah Rodmell, all of which involved the use, or suspected use, of stockings.

As to what else was said, and what was shared, in other interviews, there is no way of knowing unless police decide to make the transcripts public. It is quite possible something said in one of the conversations could have informed another probe in a significant way. It's highly unlikely the results of later interviews were shared with the teams who had already conducted their questioning.

Modern investigations into British serial killers have set a clear precedent. In 2008, a murderer emerged whose list of suspected, but unproven, victims eclipsed even that of Patrick Mackay's. Peter Tobin was a child rapist who had already served ten years for attacking two 14-year-old girls in 1993. Tobin held the youngsters at knifepoint in his home, before stabbing one, sexually assaulting them both and leaving them for dead after turning on gas taps. Fortunately, both girls survived.

Angelika Kluk was not so lucky. In 2006, the 23-year-old Polish student was staying at the presbytery of St Patrick's Church, in Anderston, Glasgow, where Tobin, then 60, was working as a handyman under the alias Pat McLaughlin. Tobin raped and murdered Angelika before hiding her body underneath the floor, close to the confession box. He then went on the run, hiding out in London. When he was arrested six weeks later, he denied murder and took the case to trial, after which he was sentenced to life with a minimum of twenty-one years.

But that was not the end of the story. Following Tobin's conviction, police in Scotland launched Operation Anagram, the first cross-force investigation into a suspected serial killer to utilize cutting edge forensic techniques and modern databases. Because of Tobin's age, and the fact that he had lived in various places across Britain, police suspected he could be linked to dozens of murders and disappearances. They dug up the body of 15-year-old Vicky Hamilton, who went missing in 1991 in Bathgate, West Lothian, where Tobin was living at the time. They also found the remains of Dinah McNicol, 18, who vanished in 1991, at another of his previous addresses in Margate, Kent. Tobin was convicted of two further counts of murder and jailed for life, without a chance of release.

Operation Anagram is ongoing, and Tobin is suspected of at least nine unsolved murders, having allegedly made cell confessions to forty-eight crimes. Criminologist David Wilson has claimed Tobin also killed three women in Glasgow in the 1960s, which were known as the 'Bible John' murders due to the assailant's habit of quoting from the Bible. Although Operation Anagram has yet to solve anything like the number of cases detectives hoped for at its outset, the decision to pool resources under one investigatory team finally brought a measure of closure for two families who had spent decades wondering what happened to their daughters. It also ensured Tobin will never be able to strike again.

A similar approach has been taken by the Metropolitan Police following the capture of another serial killer, Levi Bellfield. The former nightclub doorman was convicted in 2008 of murdering Marsha McDonnell and Amelie Delagrange, as well as the attempted murder of Kate Sheedy. He was later found guilty of murdering 13-year-old schoolgirl Milly Dowler in 2002. He was also suspected of killing up to ten other victims, including his 14-year-old childhood girlfriend, and carrying out the notorious hammer attack on Lin Russell and her daughter Megan, which saw the wrong man convicted. Bellfield is said to have made a number of cell confessions to these crimes. Although police — working in conjunction with ten other forces — later said there was no evidence to tie him to any of the unsolved crimes, they were at least investigated fully with officers having access to all the relevant files. Bellfield is thought to have made some of the false confessions in part to inflict pain on the families. Unlike Mackay, he will certainly die in prison.

The investigation into the Mackay case was not structured like Operation Anagram or the probe into Levi Bellfield. It was disjointed, with each murder squad taking turns at grilling Mackay over the crimes committed on their own doorsteps. As soon as he was convicted of three counts of manslaughter, investigations effectively ceased. In comparison, even though Tobin and Bellfield were already convicted and serving life sentences, investigations continued, resulting in further life sentences and a feeling of justice for their victims' families.

With Mackay, prosecutors did not even pursue cases for which he had already been charged. Why not? One obvious but unpalatable explanation is that it was simply too embarrassing. Serious security breaches at Ashford Remand Centre would have to be proved in order to land a conviction in the Mary Hynes case. It is highly unlikely prison bosses would have offered up any information to back the Crown's case that Mackay had been able to leave the centre and then stroll back in. And if it was proved in court, there is no telling how far the blame might have gone; a ministerial head might have rolled.

But why was the Frank Goodman case not pursued when, by all accounts, there was a confession and physical evidence tying Mackay to it? Having dropped the Mary Hynes case for practical reasons, it might well be that the authorities saw an inherent risk in having to explain why they pursued one but not the other. It was, perhaps, easier to say continuing the inquiries was not in the public interest because Mackay was already going to be locked up for a significant period of time. With few relatives on hand to complain, it was not a difficult decision to make. With that scenario in mind, it is hardly surprising that there was little appetite for an overarching investigation into all of the murders for which Mackay was questioned. But things are different now: the scope for institutional embarrassment has been diminished by the passage of time and many of those involved are dead.

Two things could happen before Mackay takes any secrets to his grave. The easiest option is for the police to continue to discount his involvement in this litany of unsolved murders, only occasionally digging out his files as a matter of bureaucratic routine. Some of the families may well be content with this approach and be happy to let sleeping dogs lie.

The second option is to allow a single force, or a team of trusted private investigators, examine all the Mackay files in a bid to determine which, if any, of the outstanding allegations would stand any chance in front of a jury, perhaps with new forensic evidence. Maybe Mackay, now older and calmer, should be re-interviewed. If there is enough evidence, it must be in the public interest to bring a prosecution. If there is not, then the hunt for the real killer, or killers, should continue.

It is fitting to end on this extract from Mackay's prison memoir, written on 3 October 1975:

> 'I feel terrible about what happened all the more because I do not know why or what made me do it. I find it all a confusing matter. You see, I'm scared of myself. At times I often try to wonder why, but it's just plain hell. Everyone with the experience I had of mishandling and brutality of the homes, remand homes, approved schools, reception centres and any other bloody place will know that the general attitude prevalent in the early and middle 1960s was vastly against the person concerned. Namely, if his or her family had no backing to speak of — such as I for instance, just a widowed mother and a very young sister — the young persons could be manipulated like a ruddy puppet on a string from pillar to post. Had I a father they would never have stood a bloody chance in Hades of manipulating me in this way. But then come to that it would never have taken place.'

More than forty years after Mackay's descent into Hell, now could be the final opportunity for the man known as the Devil's Disciple to take one last shot at redemption.

Bibliography

In addition to documents from the National Archives and private collections, this book has drawn on the following sources:

Books

Bronson, C. (2015) *Charlie Bronson Stole My Sanity.* Self published.

Clark, T., Penycate, J. (1976) *Psychopath: The Case of Patrick Mackay.* Routledge and Kegan Paul.

King, B. (1996) *Lustmord: The Writings and Artifacts of Murderers.* Bloat Books.

Morris, J. (2015) *The Who's Who of British Crime: In the 20th Century.* Amberley Publishing.

Ronson, J. (2011) *The Psychopath Test.* Picador.

Wansell, G. (2011) *The Bus Stop Killer.* Penguin.

Wilson, D. (2009) *A History of British Serial Killing.* Sphere.

Wilson, D., Harrison, P. (2010) *The Lost British Serial Killer: Closing the Case on Peter Tobin and Bible John.* Sphere.

Documentaries

Goff, G. (2013) *Born to Kill: The Devil's Disciple.* Extreme Entertainment, Sky.

Day, J., Dineage, F. (2012) *Murder Casebook: Patrick Mackay.* Woodcut Media.

Jones, N. (2002) *London's Scariest Mysteries: Patrick Mackay.* ITV.

Weissbloom, H (1989) *40 Minutes: Danger Men.* BBC.

Index